Kate Figes is the author of two best-selling works of non-fiction *Life After Birth* and *The Terrible Teens – What Every Parent Needs to Know* and two novels *What About Me? – The Diaries and Emails of a Menopausal Mother and her Teenage Daughter* and *What About Me, Too?* She is books editor at *You* magazine at the Mail on Sunday and writes regularly for the *Guardian* and *Times* newspapers.

Kate Figes is the author of two best-selling works of non-fiction *Life After Birth* and *The Terrible Teens – What Every Parent Needs to Know* and two novels *What About Me? – The Diaries and Emails of a Menopausal Mother and her Teenage Daughter* and *What About Me, Too?* She is books editor at *You* magazine at the *Mail on Sunday* and writes regularly for the *Guardian* and *Times* newspapers.

The Big
Fat Bitch
Book

The Big Fat Bitch Book
for Grown-up Girls

KATE FIGES

virago

VIRAGO

First published in Great Britain in 2007 by Virago Press

Copyright © Kate Figes 2007

A CIP catalogue record for this book
is available from the British Library.

ISBN 978-1-84408-295-7

Papers used by Virago are natural, recyclable products made
from wood grown in sustainable forests and certified in accordance
with the rules of the Forest Stewardship Council.

Typeset in Goudy by M Rules
Printed and bound in Great Britain by
Clays Ltd, St Ives plc

Virago Press
An imprint of
Little, Brown Book Group
Brettenham House
Lancaster Place
London WC2E 7EN

A Member of the Hachette Livre Group of Companies

www.virago.co.uk

I dedicate this book to the person who
let their dog shit on my doorstep . . .

Contents

Introduction

If you haven't got anything nice to say about anybody; come and sit next to me.

Alice Roosevelt Longworth, embroidered
on one of her cushions

There are all sorts of different kinds of bitches, male as well as female. Hollywood bitches like to keep journalists waiting three days for interviews and insist on hair stylists and reflex-ologists at other people's expense. Minor celebrity bitches slug it out in the tabloids and political bitches knife each other in the back. Critics entertain with their bitchery, literary bitches savage each other's books in reviews and academic bitches discredit sources to bring their rivals down. There are verbally witty bitches who fill books of quotations, like Mae West and Dorothy Parker, and then there are the sadists who dare to wind and wound face-to-face. We bitch and moan when life gets complicated and we bitch about others behind their backs because few things are more interesting than other people's foibles or weaknesses.

If we defined nouns in the English language, the word 'bitch' would undoubtedly be feminine. La bitch. Never le. Men bitch too but we rarely call it that – they use sarcasm or are skilled in the art of witty put-downs or ironic wordplay. 'Bitch' has been used as a form of insult for a woman since the fourteenth century but it was only applied to a woman considered lewd or overly promiscuous. It's interesting that it was only during the twentieth century, as women began to gain more power and a sense of place in the wider world that the insult got extended to mean a 'malicious, treacherous or unpleasant woman'. The more successful women are at work, the more they are labelled as bitches when they have to make brutal decisions. The woman who refuses to go to bed with someone is swiftly put down as a 'frigid bitch' now that virginity is no longer a prerequisite for marriage and the beloved wife becomes 'that bitch' when she takes half her husband's pension at divorce.

It is the specific and subtle way that women bitch to bond with each other and then paradoxically put each other down which interests me and is the subject of this book. Bitching is an art that girls excel at. Our verbal skills can be devastating, we shoot from the lip as so many of the bitches in this book will show. 'The other day this man was making snide remarks about me not eating anything at a party,' says Marcelle D'Argy Smith, former editor of *Cosmopolitan* magazine, 'but he was obese. I could have said something but I didn't. It would be like America attacking Croydon.' At its best, bitching can be profoundly funny banter when we bitch as equals. Bitching is useful, essential even, as a cathartic release when aspects of life, work, motherhood and men are confusing or bring us down. 'There's nothing more fun than two ex-girlfriends comparing notes about the same man,' says agony aunt Virginia Ironside. 'It's not attractive and when I do it I feel guilty about it because that's not the sort of person I want to be, but it is so amusing and comforting to share with someone else all kinds of experiences that make one laugh.'

Clever bitching is far more subtle and devious than the crude mockery of sarcasm which tends, simply, to evoke the opposite – 'Don't work too hard now, will you' (when the person is dozing with their feet on the desk). Irony is crucial, as is speed of response. Winston Churchill was a grand master of the art. 'If you were my husband, I'd poison your coffee,' Lady Astor once said to him. 'My dear,' he replied, 'If you were my wife, I'd drink it.' Insults are direct put-downs while bitching is almost always indirect. It's often done behind someone's back and if they find out what's been said they cannot easily identify the bitch or retaliate. In the rare and wonderful instances when a good bitch is delivered directly, it's often at such an acute angle or with so much subtle irony that the person in the spotlight doesn't get it until it's too late to bitch back. When Margot Asquith met Jean Harlow in Hollywood, the actress kept pronouncing the 't' at the end of her name. Margot Asquith eventually grew so tired of this that she said, 'My dear, the "t" is silent, as in Harlow.'

Women can be deeply supportive of one another; but they can also kill each other with words. We understand exactly where the weaknesses of other women lie because all too often we feel weak in those areas ourselves. We all do it, there's a bitch inside each one of us just busting to get out but we find that hard to admit. We've all been the victims of vicious verbal dexterity and we've all attacked other women behind their backs or gone too far with those barbed comments, which hit friends we care about where it hurts. Amnesia clouds our memory when it comes to our own bitchy comments or actions of the past. Nobody wants to admit to being a bitch, yet we're all happy to talk about other women being bitchy. It's a taboo subject. I wanted to find out why women bitch, why they're so good at it and whether it is possible to build better defences against those comments which are meant to wound.

It wasn't long before I discovered that this would also have to be a book about female stereotypes and the way that women reinforce these notions themselves. Gossip is an important and positive social tool utilised by men and women equally. An eighteen-month study into the social interactions of a university rowing club conducted by Kevin Kniffen and David Wilson in America has found that up to two-thirds of the conversation of both sexes is gossip, with the only real difference being that men liked to talk more about themselves. Gossip equips us with crucial information about socially acceptable norms of behaviour, office politics and family tensions, that others are unwell or in trouble and in need of greater support and understanding. But when that gossip becomes slanderous, intending to put someone else down, it mutates subtly into bitching. When we express disapproval of other women by bitching about how they look/dress/behave sexually/mother we express moral superiority, we distance ourselves from similar behaviour and unwittingly reinforce stereotypical notions of how women should be.

Whenever I mentioned to women that I was writing a book about bitching, I got one of two responses. Some laughed and immediately saw the fun side and volunteered anecdotes. But with others it caused a frisson. They went dumb and shrunk horrified against the wall. I knew what they were thinking,

'Does she think I'm a bitch?' Or they questioned the political correctness of putting the more destructive tendencies of women under the microscope. 'I wouldn't want to involve myself in the cruel bit of women, they're vulnerable enough without getting at them,' said Marcelle D'Argy Smith. Yet it is precisely that vulnerability, that lack of a sense of self and place in the world that makes women feel the need to put others down. When I put the simple question 'Are mothers bitchy?' on www.mumsnet.co.uk as a thread, it provoked a torrent of strong reaction. How dare I, or a press like Virago, devoted to women, endorse stereotypical negative views of women when men are never put down as bitches? But isn't there a sense that by refusing to acknowledge that women are human and there-fore can be cruel, we endorse the very stereotypes that we need to dismantle, where women are always supposed to be good, kind and nice?

The dark side to bitching is dark indeed. It starts in the play-ground, amongst girls as young as seven or eight, and becomes a lethal weapon amongst adolescents as they compete and try to establish themselves socially and sexually. If you turn over this book and read *The Big Fat Bitch Book For Girls* you will dis-cover just how destructive and hurtful girls can be and probably recognise emotions from your own childhood. The idea for this book came from a casual comment by a sixth former at a school in London after I chaired a discussion between Carmen Callil and Lennie Goodings about Virago. When she was asked what the worst thing about going to an all-girls' school was, the sixth former replied without hesita-tion – 'The bitching.' Interviews with girls of all ages, from mixed as well as single-sex schools confirm this. Bitching forms the bedrock of teenage conversations as they try to ascertain who they are and what they want from life. 'Everyone just bitches. When you're sitting at lunch you just bitch about something or someone you don't like. That's how you start conversations,' says one thirteen-year-old.

Friendship and popularity really matters to adolescent girls and it is often the alpha girls, those who are more socially advantaged and confident, who learn to manipulate others through the power of inclusion or exclusion. The bitching subtly shifts to a form of bullying that goes well below the radar of parents and teachers, as individuals within their friendship group are targeted with repeated taunts and put-downs, evil looks, blanking and rumour spreading. It is rife in every secondary school. The victims really suffer in their isolation and if they are not helped, quickly lose confidence and self-respect. They feel as if they are somehow to blame. If only they were 'cool' enough/thin enough then maybe they would be more accepted. Feelings of hopelessness quickly translate into depression and the victim can even grow into a woman who finds it hard to extricate herself from abusive relationships. The bully loses out too. She learns the art of manipulating and humiliating others whenever she feels threatened or insecure and considers it is an acceptable way to behave because that behaviour is rarely challenged.

Female stereotypes perpetuate the status quo. Adults believe this is just how girls are – catty, bitchy, 'sticks and stones will break my bones but words will never hurt me,' yet research shows that verbal abuse cuts as deep, if not deeper than physical bullying. Physical fights are usually public, anger is released and the wounds are there for all to see. Verbal attacks are hidden, secret and deeply undermining. 'That feeling of hurt has a neural basis. Our brain registers social rejections in the very area that activates when we are hurt physically,' writes Daniel Goleman in his book *Social Intelligence*, and 'what children experience day after day sculpts neural circuitry.' Bitching is so common in our schools that it is considered normal and that's hard for a sensitive girl who finds herself at the receiving end. The legacy those verbal wounds leave can be lasting and those experiences of being either the bitch or the victim shape the type of women we become as adults.

Girls are expected to be kinder, less aggressive, and more supportive of each other. So girls learn to suppress their crueller tendencies and then let them out in even more lethal ways. Teachers and parents find it hard to believe that that sweet, articulate, clever girl could be so evil as to start a 'We hate X club' or to initiate a three-way telephone call where the victim hears horrid things said about her. Beneath that good girl façade, bitches flourish and perfect their scorpion sting. We perfect the art of girltalk in the playground to bond and form close friendships, but inevitably that usually involves talking about somebody else, who isn't there. You get much closer to a person when you share a mutual dislike for another person than you do over someone you both like. Then as adults we're well primed. We slot easily into bitch mode with other women in social situations, even with those we don't know very well. We bitch about friends by couching their problems in empathetic tones. We bitch with our eyes, scathing glances up and down their attire, Medusa's stares. We bitch by omission, 'You've bought a new dress!' or understatement, 'I quite liked her book,' and the silent treatment when family or friends offend us extends from the playground to the grave. Anything rather than honest confrontation, appraisal or generosity of spirit. We still need to exude a sense of superiority and power because so often we lack self-confidence just as we did when we were teenagers.

Some evolutionary biologists believe that the roots of bitching lie, in part, embedded deep within our gender and the reproductive imperative, for bitching is a low risk form of veiled aggression. Teenage girls tend to bitch most about aspects of appearance, sex and sexuality because they matter in the competitive mating game. Retaliation, in the unlikely event that one is discovered trying to do another woman down, will not threaten our safety and we need to stay healthy and alive to protect our young. We also need to ward off other predatory women from our polygamous men to safeguard the economic interests of our offspring given that men still earn more and provide for them, in spite of equal opportunity. But bitching is also rooted in powerlessness. In highly competitive working environments such as politics, academia or Hollywood, men and women will bitch and backstab in equal measure to get ahead. It's just that women find themselves in more vulnerable situations so much more often than men do and they still depend on men and male support in so many ways. Research shows that aggression between women becomes more direct and physical as resources get scarcer, and young women living in areas which are socially or economically disadvantaged tend to fight physically more.

When we feel vulnerable in the wider world, when it feels like our jobs, livelihood and means of success are being judged largely on the stereotypical notions of femininity such as youth, beauty and sex appeal, women often regress to school-girl behaviour and get bitchier as a learned means of defence. In industries where women thrive solely on the basis of looks and style, such as modelling, fashion and films, bitching about each other's appearance to keep one another down zooms into orbit. 'You're always worrying about things like what you look like, how your performance is going down, whether you'll get more work, and your hair and make-up because they always make you look so awful, I think they sometimes deliberately set out in hair and make-up to bring you down,' says actress and model Susie Silvey. 'The whole thing makes you neurotic, a bit like my teenage daughter is now!' Supermodels have been known to push each other off the catwalk to remain in the spotlight. Acting is a deeply competitive and insecure-making profession. A young actress (who asked that she remain name-less, fearing bitch retaliation) landed her first small film part in the 1980s. The lead role was taken by a very well-known middle-aged actress making a comeback. 'She must have felt very insecure because she went to the director and said that the scene we were doing together was totally unnecessary and could he cut us out. We shared a dressing table but she ignored me the whole time, never said "Hello" or "Goodbye." She was the star yet she felt threatened by little insignificant me. She wanted the whole screen space all to herself.'

We bitch when we feel powerless to effect change in any other way. And there is a great deal to bitch about. Women still earn less than men in every field, often even in the same job, and they dominate the low paid service sector. To succeed in the better-paid, male-dominated industries women have to work harder than men to prove themselves. And then just at the very same moment when they need to work hardest to prove themselves career-wise, they also need to find that mate who will nourish them as lovers as well as be a good father and reproduce. Then as mothers or working mothers, an entire new world of insecurity and opportunities for bitching emerges. Bringing other women down behind their backs is a powerful form of covert competition, it makes us feel better about ourselves, about everything we feel we should do as 'perfect women' but cannot manage and about everything we desire but do not have.

Discrimination on the grounds of sex and age may be illegal but it still exists. Most successful women have to distinguish themselves from the rest by being cleverer, more ruthless and more calculating than any man at the same level. And often once they reach power they are not generous to lowlier women who dare to think they could do the same and take the position from them. 'My theory is that we were a servant class for centuries, competing with each other for scant resources,' says Allison Pearson, 'and although we've moved on from that, part of us is still there. It's difficult to unwire yourself from that and to think that another woman is not going to do you down.'

Women get just as angry as men and have a great deal more to get angry about but they're not supposed to show it. Male aggression is still often considered 'natural' and valorised, while aggression in a woman can be considered unnatural, irrational, hormonal and evidence of mental instability. Men keen on preserving their own status in macho well-paid industries such as banking, taunt, use sexual harassment and undermine women with compulsory office outings to strip clubs, knowing just how difficult it is for women to react without seeming unreasonable. We only know of this because some brave women have dared to bring sexual harassment cases here and in the States. 'Men use our gender against us at work simply to eliminate half the opposition,' says psychologist Elizabeth Mapstone. 'It's an effective weapon.'

And that's just at work – add male brutality, infidelity, dishonesty and misogyny to the mix and there's enough fuel for a girl to self-combust. But often we feel that we can't do anything about it other than smile sweetly through gritted teeth. If we can't fight the status quo without appearing brazen or butch, we get angry with each other and kick the cat. Under stress, human beings seem to blame others for what they cannot handle in themselves and women do that best verbally. 'Whenever anyone feels powerless, it seems more expedient to lash out at others in the same powerless position than it is to fight the people with real power,' writes Leora Tanenbaum in her book *Catfight*. 'Besides, when a woman challenges the inner circle of men, she runs the risk of being left on the periphery. Joining with other women to fight for better working conditions is time-consuming, tiring and risky. But if a woman belittles other women, she can prove her superiority among women – and is one step closer to the inner circle of men.'

Bitching reaches its zenith among adolescent girls because that is when girls feel most insecure about who they are. All teenagers struggle with identity, but girls face additional confusion, and seemingly contradictory messages as to how they should be and behave as young women. They need to look good – feminine, thin and sexy, but they can't match the glamour of the celebrities they want to emulate. They feel sexy, modern culture is overtly sexual and yet the prevailing culture at school is that 'good' girls don't. 'Slag' is the most hurtful insult exchanged between teenage girls, as they reinforce the chaste 'good girls don't get laid' stereotype even though they are just as entitled to experiment with and enjoy sexual activity as boys. They strive to be the good, self-sacrificial, supportive and enabling person that girls are still expected to be, but they also want to achieve their ambitions and earn their own living. But that takes competitive drive, which means distinguishing yourself as either better or different to your friends, which girls tend to feel deeply uncomfortable about. They are supposed to feel empowered these days and able to achieve everything they want, but that's another pressure in itself. Supposing they can't? What if they fail?

Women bitch to bond closely with friends and then will bitch about that same friend to others when they are cross with them or upset. We bitch when we're envious, feel insecure or can't bear the idea of another woman getting ahead because life's so competitive. We bitch to fathom the darkest recesses of our sadistic tendencies. Teenage girls conduct a ritualistic power dance in schools between the bitch and the victim, that can sear permanently. It may be that rising interest in 'bad' girls – with films such as Mean Girls, books like this one and a plethora of newspaper articles about rising rates of aggression between teenagers – has highlighted something that was already there. Or it could be that young women are less scared and hemmed in by the old 'good' girl stereotypes and appear to be bitchier but are actually just more outspoken and assertive. Or it may be straight sexism, that as young women work harder and succeed, men highlight their bitchery that much more because they constitute so much more of a threat. I suspect that all of these factors play a part.

But I also know, from the countless teenagers and parents I speak to researching and writing about adolescence, that young women have a great deal more to get angry about, with raised expectations, disappointments and the stress inherent to feeling as if they have to achieve perfection in every aspect of their lives. Young women are more confident, more outspoken and more aggressive than ever before, yet the inner insecurities associated with being female, with being the 'good' girl still exist – never feeling as if you look good enough, loving food but not wanting to gain weight, sexual conduct and reputation, earning enough to be independent and marrying motherhood with work ambitions. Rising numbers of young people are finding it difficult to cope with the tasks inherent to growing up, for the statistics on depression, drink and drug abuse, eating disorders, self-harm and suicide rise each year, they don't fall. Rising rates of malicious bitching, rumour spreading and victimisation of individuals in schools are not 'just what girls do', they are yet another manifestation of stress and individual crisis and in our 'no holds barred' culture, where the lines between polite society and brutal honesty are now so blurred, young girls have little guidance as to how to behave.

Men are bitchier too, as is modern culture, with reality TV games shows like *Big Brother* and Anne Robinson's *The Weakest Link*, and magazines like *Sneak* and *Heat* which trash the famous for sweat marks or spots. Public humiliation is big entertainment these days. Celebrities such as Posh and Jordan or Kelly Osbourne and Christina Aguilera launch missiles at each other in the tabloids, others choose award ceremonies to undermine rivals, and there are plenty of examples in this book to entertain you. Teenagers lap all of this up. Exposure to the psychological weaknesses and physical inadequacies of others makes them feel better about their own. They see that many women still achieve fame for how they look rather than for what they can do and often these women have such a faint grasp on success that they have to preserve their status by putting other women down personally and that must have an infectious effect.

I conducted a small experiment, one that would not pass a single scientific trial specification but an experiment all the same. I gorged on as much of Britain's media as I could for a whole week to monitor the output. My sitting room floor sank beneath the weight of newspapers and weekly magazines – more than twenty celebrity-watch weeklies such as *Heat* and *Star* are now published on Tuesday, all with the same hazy long-distance shots – and my eyes grew glazed and bloodshot from watching television. I chose a random week – the second week in January 2006 – but it turned out to be a good one for a bitchathon. Charles Kennedy had to resign after a nasty coup instigated by his colleagues. One liberal democrat (male) stuck the boot into Sarah Kennedy for not helping her husband to overcome his alcoholism earlier on. Mohammed Al Fayed accused Alexander Chancellor of being a 'middle-class racist willing to sink to any depths to please his establishment masters' in the *Guardian*. Poor Wendi Peters of *Coronation Street* left the *Soapstar Superstar* studio in tears after judge Billy Sammeth told her on air that a 'woman of her age and stature should keep certain bits covered up'. The acting leader of the Liberal Democrats, Sir Menzies Campbell, had a disastrous first

Prime Minister's Question Time when he complained that 'one in five schools does not have a permanent head' only to be trounced seconds later by the Prime Minister's reply, that it can be 'hard to find a permanent head of an organisation if it is a failing organisation'. And two of the bitchiest worlds finally came together when politician George Galloway entered the *Big Brother* household. Interestingly men, it seemed to me, were doing most of the bitching.

By day two I was beginning to feel sick, from looking at literally dozens of pairs of tits and semi-pornographic shots of minor celebrity women in the tabloids. Serious issues such as the rest of the world rarely featured. I had also driven past several massive posters of Elizabeth Hurley standing next to a model's dummy stabbed with pairs of scissors in the back – an advert for a television programme with the words 'You can't have fashion without victims, darling'. The word 'darling' brought out the bitchiness of yet another reality TV show. By day three, after digesting the weeklies and hundreds of pages dismantling the figures and styles of celebrities with ruthless abandon, I found myself running my eyes up and down someone's perfectly ordinary skirt and thinking 'how can *she* wear *that!*' Bingo. I'm usually much too vague, preoccupied and myopic to notice anybody else's clothes unless they are worn by my children and are inappropriate or need mending. Somehow all this filth was beginning to get to me.

We are surrounded by a bitchy, bring-you-down culture and that must affect both men and women equally and make them bitchier. But I believe that female bitching is connected to our expectations of women and the conflict between the selfless 'Good Girl' paradigm and the human need to be honest, critical or cross. We ask more of other women than we do of men. We expect them to be like mothers to us, to be kinder and more giving and then when they are not, we judge them more harshly and are less willing to forgive their flaws and con-tradictions. Women are often the first to name a female boss battling to maintain her position a 'bitch', or another woman a 'slut' when she is as entitled to an active sex life as any man. We're trying to prove ourselves as equal to men in the world and the work-place and we are easily their equal. But we also don't want to lose the 'Good Girl' image and the selflessness inherent to that notion flies directly in the face of what people need to succeed – ambition, competitive drive and the ability to take criticism or be critical without causing offence.

Sometimes the 'Good Girl' is just too hard a fiction to main-tain when the odds of success in an unequal world are stacked against us. Sometimes you can't help feeling that if you can't beat the stereotypes, you might as well join them and be the bitch. For life's a bitch and then you die! When someone in the media bitches, they open a door and make it acceptable for everyone else to do the same. In this licentious culture where we're expected to express our true feelings, old-fashioned man-ners are no longer paramount. Men bitch too now, about women as they watch them rising in the ranks beside them. Boys bitch more at school, appropriating girl-style bullying because they can see it is a low-risk strategy and they are unlikely to get caught. Some gay comedians now push bitching to its limits in a way that many women find hard to take. But women still face issues, which are particular to their gender. When you marry this cultural shift with the fact that women are now expected to attain perfection in so many aspects of their lives – work, marriage, motherhood, modelling fabulous clothes on a stick thin body – we shouldn't be surprised if women bitch more, just as they drink more as a cathartic release.

Women are supposed to be all things now, to have it all, but such expectations are fraught with contradictions. She wants to look good, but she loves to eat. She wants to be noticed and stand out as distinct from other women, yet she craves the approval and admiration of other women most. She wants to be a good and supportive friend to her girlfriends, a good lover, a good mother and a good daughter, but we also need to behave more like the boys if we want to get ahead. Instead of rejecting the 'Good Girl' image and raging at the world, which seems to want so much from us, we blame ourselves for not being strong enough to hack it, and bitch about those women who give the impression that they can accomplish all of this with ease.

We admire the chutzpah of strong, self-assured women like Madonna, Katharine Hepburn, Germaine Greer and Sharon Osbourne because they have achieved something in their own right and flout conventions of good female behaviour. Strong women are honest about who they are, their strengths and failings and what they want from life. They're not afraid to show that they sweat. When they're labelled as 'bitchy' it's in the most positive sense, for bitch means Being In Total Control Honey. The 'Bitch Ph.D.' website defines it as follows: 'There are people out there who *don't* hate women, but who *do* feel acutely uncomfortable around "bitchy" women. That is, women who don't ask for permission before speaking; women who don't just state their opinion and then back off to let you decide if you want to hear it or not, but who insist on having their arguments acknowledged; women who feel entitled to be angry; women who want to be heard more than they want to be liked.'

Clever bitching is thrilling, it takes us to places we feel we shouldn't go, an extreme female sport that is often very funny. We love to distinguish ourselves and show others that we don't care what they think of us. When people bitch they show daring and expose truths which good manners dictate we shouldn't reveal. But at its worst, bitching can be deeply hurtful and that the line between wit and cruelty can be so very fine it is almost invisible. 'I have been described as rude,' Bette Davis once said. 'Well I don't think I'm rude. I certainly never *wished* to be cruel. But I have never had time for affecting foolish manners. It always seemed more honest not to.'

There are ways to bitch well, to revel in the pleasure of wordplay and girlplay without hurting others. Real women are not demure, always kind, self-sacrificing and never cross. They're loud, outspoken, clever, daring, funny and strong. When women find the courage to be themselves rather than pander to female stereotypes, they discover a strength they never knew they had, a confidence they need to flourish in this world. They become the best type of bitch. I hope this book (both sides of it) will show you how.

~

Emma
by Jane Austen

They had a very fine day for Box Hill . . . At first it was downright dullness to Emma. She had never seen Frank Churchill so silent and stupid. He said nothing worth hearing – looked without seeing – admired without intelligence – listened without knowing what she said. While he was so dull, it was no wonder that Harriet should be dull likewise; and they were both insufferable.

When they all sat down it was better; to her taste a great deal better, for Frank Churchill grew talkative and gay, making her his first object. Every distinguishing attention that could be paid, was paid to her. To amuse her, and be agreeable in her eyes, seemed all that he cared for – and Emma, glad to be enlivened, not sorry to be flattered, was gay and easy too, and gave him all the friendly encouragement, the admission to be gallant, which she had ever given in the first and most animating period of their acquaintance; but which now, in her own estimation, meant nothing, though in the judgement of most people looking on, it must have had such an appearance as no English word but flirtation could very well describe . . .

'I saw you first in February. Let everybody on the Hill hear me if they can. Let my accents swell to Mickleham on one side and Dorking on the other. I saw you first in February.' And then whispering – 'Our companions are excessively stupid. What shall we do to rouse them? Any nonsense will serve. They *shall* talk. Ladies and

Gentlemen, I am ordered by Miss Woodhouse (who, wherever she is, presides) to say, that she desires to know what you are all thinking of.' Some laughed, and answered good-humouredly. Miss Bates said a great deal; Mrs Elton swelled at the idea of Miss Woodhouse's presiding; Mr Knightley's answer was the most distinct.

'Is Miss Woodhouse sure that she would like to hear what we are all thinking of?'

'Oh! No, no' cried Emma, laughing as carelessly as she could 'upon no account in the world. It is the very last thing I would stand the brunt of just now. Let me hear anything rather than what you are all thinking of. I will not say quite all. There are one or two, perhaps, (glancing at Mr Weston and Harriet), whose thoughts I might not be afraid of knowing.'

'It is a sort of thing,' cried Mrs Elton emphatically, 'which I should not have thought myself privileged to inquire into. Though, perhaps, as the *chaperon* of the party – I never was in any circle – exploring parties – young ladies – married women –'

Her mutterings were chiefly to her husband; and he murmured, in reply.

'Very true, my love, very true. Exactly so, indeed – quite unheard of – but some ladies say anything. Better pass it off as a joke. Everybody knows what is due to *you*.'

'It will not do,' whispered Frank to Emma, 'they are most of them affronted. I will attack them with more address. Ladies and gentlemen – I am ordered by Miss Woodhouse to say, that she waves her right of knowing exactly what you may all be thinking of and only requires something very entertaining from each of you, in a general way. Here are seven of you, besides myself (who, she is pleased to say, am very entertaining already) and she only demands from each of you either one thing very clever – or two things moderately clever – or three things very dull indeed, and she engages to laugh heartily at them all.'

'Oh! Very well,' exclaimed Miss Bates, 'Then I need not be uneasy. "Three things very dull indeed." That will do just for me, you know. I shall be sure to say three dull things as soon as ever I open my mouth, shan't I? – (looking round with the most good-humoured dependence on every body's assent) – Do not you all think I shall?'

Emma could not resist.

'Ah! Ma'am, but there may be a difficulty. Pardon me – but you will be limited as to number – only three at once.'

Miss Bates, deceived by the mock ceremony of her manner, did not immediately catch her meaning; but when it burst on her, it could not anger, though a slight blush showed that it could pain her.

Rival Screen Queens

It's a new low for actresses when you have to wonder what's between her ears instead of her legs.

Katharine Hepburn on Sharon Stone

~

Go to the Martin Beck Theatre and watch Katharine Hepburn run the gamut of emotions from A to B.

Dorothy Parker on her performance in *The Lake*

Hepburn replied:
Extremely funny and accurate.

~

The word 'great' stands for something. When you talk about a great actor you're not talking about Tom Cruise.

Lauren Bacall

~

A great band like that and they have to play with Ella. That bitch!

Billie Holiday

Female stars are acutely vulnerable. There is always someone younger, more beautiful and equally talented out there who could knock them off their perch. Hollywood stars notoriously wield their power by making others wait or run around them, demanding hair-stylists and reflexologists and reneging on promises at the last minute. However, the legendary bitch battle between Joan Crawford and Bette Davis towers high above the rest. For four decades, these formidable goddesses fought a vicious and prolonged public battle over the top star slot, men, money, Academy Award nominations, charitable donations and motherhood, as well as coveted film roles. When Bette Davis gave birth to her daughter, Crawford adopted two more children. When Davis was nominated for an Oscar for *Whatever Happened to Baby Jane* and Crawford wasn't, the latter approached the other foreign nominees to enquire if, in their absence, she could accept the award on their behalf. When Anne Bancroft got the award for Best Actress, it was Crawford who got to walk onto the stage to accept the award and not Bette Davis. When Crawford joined Warner Brothers in 1943, she was given the choice of three dressing rooms. She chose the one next to Bette Davis, where they even fought over choice of music. Crawford played classical records by Isaac Stern; Davis retaliated with loud boogie-woogie until someone sneaked into their trailers and cut the wires to their machines. In *Whatever Happened to Baby Jane*, the only film they ever starred in together, when it came to the scene where Davis had to lift the ailing Crawford out of bed and carry her out of the room, Crawford put on a heavy lead-lined belt beneath her clothes, revenge for the three stitches Crawford needed in her head when Davis kicked her particularly hard in one scene. Crawford fought mainly through underhand tactics; Davis asserted the upper hand with words. But as Rival Queens, with star images to maintain, their squabbles and major skirmishes were kept carefully concealed for many years. Until the early 1970s when Shaun Considine, a wandering cub reporter from County Clare, Ireland, received a telephone call from Bette Davis. During their conversation. Miss Davis suddenly segued into a conversation about Joan Crawford's unprofessionalism during the making of *Whatever Happened to Baby Jane?*. A few days later he received a call from Miss Crawford who insisted on giving her side of the turbulent story. 'For years Davis and Crawford went to considerable lengths to downplay or deny that there was any bad blood between them,' he writes in the preface to his hugely enjoyable book on their rivalry. 'Now I knew first hand that the feud not only existed, it was ready to erupt, bursting into full flame at the mere mention of the other star's name.' The material above and the quotes below are taken from his book *Bette and Joan – the Divine Feud*. They were brilliant actresses and the screen was big enough for both of them.

What in the hell did she ever contribute to fashion – except those goddamned shoulder-pads and those tacky fuck-me shoes?

Davis on Crawford when she was quoted as a major influence on '30's and '40s fashion

~

She slept with every male star at MGM except Lassie.

Davis, when told of Crawford's vast popularity with men

~

'Bette Davis is disappointed with life', said Joan, 'That's why if you look at her mouth carefully, darling, you'll see that it has turned down.'

~

'How *wonderful*,' said Bette Davis when told of Crawford's plans to play Shakespeare. 'We are all so thrilled that Joan has learned how to read.'

~

When Crawford joined Warner Brothers, Jack Warner rang Davis to tell her. 'How *nice* for you Jack,' she replied. 'Are you planning on making some more musicals for the war?'

~

When Crawford won an Oscar for *Mildred Pierce*, Davis sent her a telegram saying simply 'Congratulations.'

'Isn't that sweet,' said Joan. 'There is no feud. My heart is too full. Certainly there is room for both of us at Warner's.'

'When hell freezes over,' was Davis's reply when told of this comment.

~

When Davis was nominated for Best Actress for *All About Eve*, Crawford, who had expected a nomination for *Harriet Craig*, was not mentioned. She was suddenly ill and cancelled her appearance at the Photoplay Awards dinner. During the evening Davis waved her cigarette at an adjoining table –

'Who is that little boy seated between Ann Blyth and Elizabeth Taylor? He keeps staring in my face.'

That was Joan Crawford's nine-year-old son Christopher she was told. He was accepting the award that night for his mother.

'How *sweet*,' said Davis, 'and where is Joan?'

'At home ill,' was the answer.

'Oh,' said Bette, 'something fatal, I hope.'

~

I love the new poodle-cut hairstyles for women. I saw stripper Lili St Cyr wearing one in her act at Ciro's. I went out the next day and got the same style.

Bette Davis

~

Those new poodle hair-dos are not for elderly
women. I think they look better on dogs and
teenagers. I should know, I have one of each.

Joan Crawford

In the film *The Star*, Davis modelled herself on Joan
Crawford and received excellent reviews. Davis received
an Oscar nomination for the role, but placed one slot
ahead of her was Crawford for *Sudden Fear*. 'I am
honoured to be in the same company as Julie Harris and
Shirley Booth,' said Crawford, ignoring the other two
nominees Susan Hayward and Davis. 'Of course, I had
heard that she was supposed to be playing me,' she said
years later, 'but I don't believe it. Did you see the picture?
It couldn't possibly be me. Bette looked so old and so
dreadfully overweight.'

'Why do I have to look so damn old?' Crawford
said after viewing the early dailies on *Whatever
Happened to Baby Jane*. 'It's like I have a
grandmother playing my part.'

'Joan, if you're so unhappy with this film,' replied
Davis, 'I'll play your part and you'll play mine.'

Crawford broke down and wept, 'I can't play *her*.
She's twice as ugly.'

Bette Davis did her own make-up on *Whatever Happened
to Baby Jane*. She didn't trust the make-up men to go as far

as she would. 'It was important that the make-up show the desperation. Miss Crawford wanted to look as nice as she could. I wanted to look as terrible as I could. Miss Crawford was a glamourpuss. I was an actress.'

On the third week of filming *Whatever Happened to Baby Jane*, both Crawford and Davis published their autobiographies. Joan had the 'makings of a good book in her', said Bette, 'but this *isn't* it'; and Crawford observed that her rival's memoirs were depressing – due largely again to the lack of attractive, virile men in her life. 'Poor Bette,' said Joan. 'It appears she's never had a happy day – or night – in her life.' '*Whaaaaatt!*' said Bette on hearing that. 'I've had affairs; not as many as her, but outside of a cathouse, who has?'

Sure, she stole some of my big scenes, but the funny thing is, when I see the movie again, she stole them because she looked like a parody of herself, and I still looked like something of a star.

Joan Crawford

~

They were like two Sherman tanks, openly despising one another.

Robert Aldrich, their director on
Whatever Happened to Baby Jane?

~

She has a cult but what the hell is a cult except a gang of rebels without a cause. I have *fans*. There's a big difference.

Joan Crawford

~

I'm so at peace with the world that I'm even thinking good thoughts about Bette Davis, Crawford wrote on one of her Christmas cards. Five months later when was told of Joan Crawford's death in 1977 she said, 'You should never say bad things about the dead, you should only say good . . . Joan Crawford is dead, good!'

Quotes from *Bette and Joan – The Divine Feud* by Shaun Considine (All rights retained by author)

~

She looks like something that would eat its young.

Dorothy Parker on Dame Edith Evans

~

If Cher has another face-lift she'll be wearing a beard.

Jennifer Saunders

~

Is Elizabeth Taylor fat? Her favourite food is seconds.

Joan Rivers

~

Elizabeth Taylor has more chins than the Chinese telephone directory.

Joan Rivers

~

Elizabeth Taylor is so fat that when she pierces her ears gravy comes out.

Joan Rivers

Joan Rivers has said in an interview that when she first began lampooning Elizabeth Taylor, she inquired about her feelings through a mutual friend Roddy McDowell. The following message came back, 'Tell her it doesn't get me where it hurts at all.' To be fair to Rivers, she is also just as damning and just as self-denigrating when it comes to her own image with lines such as 'I wish I had a twin so that I could know what I'd look like without plastic surgery,' and 'My best birth control now is to leave the lights on.'

Bitchland

In a mixed school the girls are trying to impress the boys, but in a girls' school it's just bitchland.

Debbie, fourteen

It starts at school with the distinctly different ways that girls and boys play, compete and bond with one another. Both sexes are keenly aware of the social order of their peer groups but have different ways of establishing their own position. Boys like challenge and target setting, who can throw stones or piss the furthest, and they are happy with a hierarchical structure where the top dog is admired for his sporting prowess. They express their aggression and competitive spirit in healthier ways, within clearly defined rules as participants or spectators of team sports. 'Boys rank each other through play, from pitching pennies to baseball and flying kites,' says the American anthropologist Marjorie Harness Goodwin, who has studied gender differences in play. 'Girls spend a lot more time evaluating the activities of other people, reading the social scene, who's in and who's out. They enjoy it.'

Girls compete with each other covertly over looks, clothes and material possessions, aspects of 'self' which are defined genetically and by socio-economic circumstances and are harder to influence or change. 'There's always this silent competition,' says Amanda, who is fifteen. 'If you go to a party and you think you've got this really nice outfit, there'll be someone there with a better outfit, so you'll want to bitch about her.' At a recent adult party in our house, four twelve-year-old girls amused themselves for most of the evening by discussing who had the best/worst haircut, the nicest/ugliest shoes. It's hard to imagine four twelve-year-old boys doing the same. When I asked them about their conclusions the following morning, I marvelled at their acute perceptions. They were right. They were also very funny about it. As we grow older, that judging skill matures too. It tunes into the hidden meanings of other people's behaviour, their love-lives, their hang-ups, their mistakes. 'I think we define ourselves not by who we are, but by who we are not,' says psychologist Anne Campbell. 'If I accuse someone else of being "snobby", then I am clearly implying that I am not.'

Tween culture has invaded girlhood and female rivalry seems to be beginning earlier. Many of the age-old games which encouraged sharing have disappeared and unsupervised outdoor play, where children learn to socialise with a wide range of other children, is now rare outside school. Instead they spend hours watching television alone or reaching out to others on MSN or text from the isolation of their homes. Girls as young as six and seven channel their competitive energy into their appearance, into make-up and nail varnish and forming clubs which exclude others, terrorist training camps for the verbal war that erupts during adolescence. When boys fall out they tend to focus on less personal issues to resolve their disputes, with fighting or arm-wrestling, where there are clear winners and losers. Other boys stand clear of the action and allow them to resolve it themselves. Girls attack each other personally and in less obvious ways, bystanders pitch in confusing the issues and the war rumbles on for months.

Girls are also less happy with a hierarchy in their friendship groups. They form much more intimate relationships with each other than boys do and their loyalty first and foremost is to their friends. They prefer cooperative play, with everyone on much the same level, and will pull back anyone they consider to be too 'spoilt', 'bossy', 'vain' or 'up-themselves' by bitching about them with others behind their backs. Girls who attempt to shine make other girls feel inadequate and bitching about them helps to strengthen alliances as a group. 'When you bitch to boys about girls it goes over their heads, they don't understand it,' says Juliet, who is fifteen, 'but with girls if you tell them something it goes into their brains and they think "How can I use this? Who can I tell?" They can also be reasonably certain that sooner or later their criticisms or complaints will get back to the person without them knowing who actually said it. When boys want to insult each other they tend to wind each other up with blatant untruths as if it were some sort of jocular sport, a macho display of feather rustling. Girls will do anything rather than insult each other to their faces because when they do, it's usually true and therefore so hurtful that they risk losing that friendship forever.

Children are learning about themselves and the world around them every minute of every day. They have few social skills and begin to understand how to get on with each other through a tortuous process of trial and error in densely-packed schools where they cannot avoid each other's irritations. Girls tend to have more advanced verbal and psycho-social skills, which they use to manipulate others for the power and secure sense of self that comes with popularity. They bitch because group judgements provide them with crucial guidance as to how to look and behave when they feel so vulnerable about who they are or how they should be. But they also bitch about each other to deflect attention from their own weaknesses. The more unhappy they are either at home or school, the more they will bitch about others to defend themselves. The bossiest or most attention-seeking girl in a gang of friends is usually the one who feels the most insecure. She has to shout the loudest to make her views heard and needs the affirmation that comes from being listened to, with her advice followed. If that unhappiness is extreme, because of emotional abuse or neglect, the bitching can turn into a vicious and pernicious form of bullying, another 'acting out' manifestation of a child in distress. 'When girls have really bad and stressful issues to deal with at home, they let it out at school,' says Margaret Clark, who has been a youth worker based in schools in North Wales for the past ten years. 'When girls bitch to bully it's often an expression of severe problems, just like eating disorders or self-harm.'

Astonishingly, most studies of bullying in children up until 1992 were of boys. Stereotypical gender assumptions simply ruled girls out of the equation. Catty or bitchy comments were just part of their natural make-up, children can be very cruel, it's 'what girls do', and the impact was considered minimal compared to the physical damage that boys could inflict on one another. Then a group of Norwegian researchers published the first research paper on aggression in girls – 'Of Mice and Women – Aspects of Female Aggression' (Academic Press

1992) which showed that girls express their anger against each other in very different ways to boys and that bitching about others is a prime weapon in their arsenal, particularly from the ages of ten to fourteen. Since then more research has been conducted, mainly on white, middle-class girls, and we now have a new term for this form of female bullying 'relational aggression'. Rachel Simmons defines it in her book *Odd Girl Out* as 'ignoring someone to punish them or get one's own way, excluding someone socially for revenge, using negative body language or facial expressions, sabotaging someone else's relationships, or threatening to end a relationship unless the friend agrees to a request.' It's all done well beneath the radar of teachers and adults. 'Covert aggression isn't just about not getting caught; half of it is looking like you'd never mistreat someone in the first place,' writes Rachel Simmons. 'They pass covert looks and notes, manipulate quietly over time, corner one another in hallways, turn their backs, whisper and smile. These acts, which are intended to escape detection and punishment, are epidemic in middle-class environments where the rules of femininity are more rigid, where characteristics such as being kind, generous, selfless, sweet and accommodating are nurtured above all else.'

Mention these tactics to any girl over the age of ten and she will know what you are talking about. In fact, I now know from talking to women about bitching for this book that most women who have been educated at school will recognise the syndrome. Popularity is the most important currency in every year group, in every school and the 'Queen Bees' as Rosalind Wiseman has termed them, will do anything to maintain their position. Sometimes it takes the form of an openly public humiliation – the popular eleven-year-old who went up to an unpopular girl and asked her whether she was busy this week-end. When the unpopular girl replied that she didn't know, (she didn't want to let on that she had no plans), the popular girl replied, 'Too bad, because we're going skating and we wanted you to come.' The unpopular girl then said, 'Oh . . . Well, maybe I can come,' to which the popular girl said, turning to the others, 'Oh, listen to that! She thought I meant it!' The popular girl highlighted the other girl as both unpopular *and* stupid enough to think that they would ask her out. More often, girls engage in alliance building, making it quite clear that someone is 'out', without anyone ever telling them what they have done to cause such offence. They hide behind the gang, not wanting to risk losing an ounce of popularity by being identified as the perpetrator. 'You want to seem perfect so you pretend to like them and then when they go, you just like have this massive bitch about them with your friends,' says Jemima, who is fourteen. 'You'd lose your power if you said anything to them face-to-face because you've said "you're really annoying me" and then they can do whatever they like and go and bitch about you.'

When people feel good about themselves and their sense of place in the world they tend to be nicer to each other. Aggressive behaviour increases when people feel helpless or powerless. A recent study by Yale University found that participants spread good gossip about a third party when they felt accepted in a group, but made derogatory remarks when they felt marginalized. It's an animal instinct. Primatologist Frans de Waal has found that apes and monkeys bully lower ranking members of the group when the group is under strain or when the hierarchy is threatened. Packs of wolves bully the 'omega', the weakling with low status at the bottom of the pack, who is used as a punchbag. Identifying another victim unifies the group and protects other members of that group from ostracism, James Garbarino, author of *And Words Can Hurt Forever*, says.

We may appear to be adult, but we all resort to those same playground tactics when we feel threatened, trashing innocent strangers for their appearance to friends out of earshot, name-dropping or talking about glamorous parties that we know others haven't been invited to, spreading gossip about someone we don't trust not to stab us in the back at work, or flattering people with obvious insincerity. Men do this too.

Anne is the youngest of three sisters and their mother never concealed from any of them that Anne was her favourite child. When their father died and her mother became ill in her eighties, Anne went in to look after her three times a day for the last four years of her life. 'My sisters seemed to resent it, and wouldn't help me to help her. Then when she died it got really nasty over money. My husband and I had bought my mother's flat for her twenty years earlier, which they knew, but they implied that I had forced our mother to sign something to say that the flat was ours. Her will split everything three ways, except for the flat which we had paid for, but there was this huge fuss about it.' Then six months later, Anne got an email from her nephew, which had been sent, he maintained, to everyone on her sister's address book *by accident*. 'It went on and on so hatefully about how my mother didn't love any of them except me and that his mother had been sent a whole load of junk and look where all of the money had gone, and the flat . . . it really really hurt me. Lots of people who received the message emailed back to say ignore it, but how could you? My nephew then e-mailed me, not to apologise but to say that I wasn't meant to read it, the implication being that somehow we were in the wrong for reading it.' It is the sort of tactic employed by adolescent girls, on MSN – hurtful comments that they are rarely brave enough to say directly. Anne's nephew had vented his spleen by pressing the 'reply all' button accidentally on purpose.

It's hard not to gasp at the prolonged childish tactics employed by four women and one man at a large city bank against one of their colleagues, Helen Green, reported in the *Guardian* (2/8/2006) after her successful action in the High Court. They 'blanked' her from day one. One of the women joked that she could smell a stink and held her nose and blew raspberries whenever Helen Green walked across the room. The campaign against her escalated, spreading through departments to men as well as to women over the next four years. She had to lock work away to stop it from going missing. Her name was removed from the global intranet directory and from departmental circulation lists, and the bullying became so stressful she ended up having not one nervous breakdown but two. She had suffered abuse as a child from her adopted father and simply wasn't strong enough to take what many consider to be standard office bullying. That Helen Green was brave enough to take her employers to court was not what concerned much of the press surrounding her victory. They condemned her for not being tough enough to take it. Playground bullying, where individuals are ostracised, teased and humiliated is condoned because it is so common.

The emphasis is on the victim who has to toughen up and not on the mob for their behaviour.

We may get better at masking the way we compare ourselves to other women as we grow up, but we still do it, slotting them into an invisible pecking order. At the Orange Prize party in 2006 I was talking to two lovely women writers. Another author approached, looked at each of us in turn and then walked away. My unbitchy husband would interpret that generously – she must be very short-sighted. If I hadn't been absorbed in this topic for months I would probably have agreed with him. Now I would call that bitchy, for all three of us have now clocked a judgement about her as a person as a result. Instead of running her eyes up and down our bodies to see what we were wearing or whether we had put on weight, she looked at our faces, felt we weren't interesting or useful enough, and walked off without even a smile. But then it was a 'women's' event where woman were being pitted competitively against each other as writers. Whenever women are massed together in schools, on the catwalk, at women's magazines, they seem to bring out the worst in each other as well as the best. The notion that only one woman can triumph lives on or as Phyllis Chesler, author of *Woman's Inhumanity to Woman* puts it, 'There can only be one queen, one Miss America, one wife.'

Hillary Brittan is a psychotherapist. She spent eighteen months with the women of Greenham, who camped outside the military base to prevent the arrival of cruise missiles in the early 1980s. She says there were distinct cliques and hierarchies, with the lesbians and those who had been to prison at the top. It was deeply supportive as women together but at times it was also very bitchy. 'I lived at the green gate, but we were not as powerful as the orange gate where all the luminaries who made a career out of it lived, and all the young dykes were at the blue gate. It was a tough place to live and you had to be very tough to survive – and like any organisation under stress it broke down at times. They were verbally abusive to the men who brought us essential things but they were happy to take their goodies. They treated them with scorn and disdain. It was embarrassing. And then there were vicious denunciations, with women accusing each other of heinous things like not sharing food or pulling their weight or revealing secrets. These may have been true but they could have been handled in a nicer way. Have you read that book *Queen Bees and Wannabes*? It was just like that, only these were supposed to be grown ups.'

You've Got a Friend

MARGO CHANNING: You bought the new girdles a size
  smaller, I can feel it.
BIRDIE: Something maybe grew a size larger.
MARGO CHANNING: When we get home you're going to
  get into one of those girdles and act for two-and-a-half
  hours.
BIRDIE: I couldn't get into the girdle in two-and-a-half
  hours.

From *All About Eve*

It's the friends you can call up at 4 am that matter.

Marlene Dietrich

Men, motherhood and marriage may come and go but it is our friendships with other women that can last a lifetime. They give us the sustenance and support we need to get through life as women. They *understand*. The only place where you can really let rip and bitch (moan) about the female predicament is with another woman. We bond intimately and share secrets and strategies to help each other survive and juggle life's difficulties. We drop everything to rally to a close friend in trouble.

We exchange intimacies with our closest girlfriends that we wouldn't consider sharing even with lovers. 'Put us together and there's no stopping us,' writes Fay Weldon in her book *What Makes Women Happy*. 'Listen in to any female conversation: the talk and laughter at a girls' night out. Anecdotes about the follies of men and jokes about the minimal size of their parts. Tales of male vanity and self-delusion. Their stumbling mumble-ness, their crazy driving.'

It's the intense, sublime quality of our talk that binds us together so forcefully. Gossip is not tittle-tattle for idle and mainly female minds. We all do it, it's our collective unconscious, our social glue. It's just that once again there are different gendered terms for it. At the largely male world of work or work functions, it's networking; at the school gate or social functions which are intended purely for pleasure, it's just gossip. Networking is positively encouraged and good for business; gossip is considered poisonous and pernicious. Maybe there isn't much difference between the two beyond the genders they're associated with? Women were the original networkers, trading everything from cooking and health tips within the community and passing those secrets down from mother to daughter. Gossip equips us with the knowledge that others are in trouble and in need of support and greater understanding and it is through gossip that we establish a moral blueprint for our lives. Research consistently shows that two-thirds of all conversations both at work and at home and irrespective of gender are devoted to the social aspects of our lives. We're riveted by the details of accident, illness, death and divorce because we're all vulnerable to them. And while some gossip is indeed malicious, most of it has positive intent as we search for closeness, more intimate links with one another and solutions to personal or familial difficulties.

It is because women are so good at confiding and talking cogently about their emotional lives that they form such firm, close, lifelong friendships. We support each other that much more intimately by paying compliments, and offering reassurance and deep empathy when things go wrong. And that's good for us. Good social relationships can help to strengthen the immune system, reduce the risks of depression and speed recovery from surgery. Scientists in Adelaide, Australia even believe that good social relationships could help us live longer. They studied 1500 people over the age of seventy for a decade and found that those in the top third of good social networks were 22 per cent less likely to die even if they'd also been through major stress like the death of a spouse. (http://news.bbc.co.uk/1/hi/health/4094632.stm) We need to talk after a trauma to make sense of it and lessen the blow. We gather friends from every port – school, university, work, neighbours, our children's playgroups and schools, book clubs. When those friendships are established fabulous bitching banter emerges. With our oldest, closest friends we can let the bad girl out and laugh. The broadcaster Gill Pyrah has been friends with Susan Marling for decades. During her David Bowie phase during the 1980s, Gill had an all-in-one pale blue space suit with a metallic lining. When Susan saw her wearing it at a party she said, 'Lovely. And you're oven ready.' My dear friend Fanny phoned me one day to tell me about an exciting project ghosting a book by a minor pop star. 'You won't tell anyone, will you?' 'Of course not,' I replied. And then back it came, 'It's okay, you don't know anyone that interesting.' And I laughed like a drain.

Both of these statements could have hurt, for there is such a fine line between laughter and tears when we feel vulnerable or insecure. Women can be acutely sensitive and tend to outscore men in tests on empathy and understanding what would be a faux pas in a given social situation. We read each other's eyes, searching for intuitive knowledge about what they might be thinking or feeling. We read between the lines and look for hidden meanings. 'Women are more sensitive to the innuendo of what's being said,' says social psychologist Terri Apter. 'Men are usually less sensitive to the range of emotions, particularly in a domestic setting, so they don't fight back or refine bitchy retorts in the same way.'

Often we get it right, but we can take it badly by being over-sensitive to what's being said, taking offence when we could do ourselves a favour by shoring up our sense of self enough to simply take the comment, laugh and bat it back. Susie Silvey told me that when she bumped into an old friend at a party she tried to pay a compliment by saying, 'How lovely your hair looks, it looks so thick – it used to look a bit sparse but now it just looks so amazing.' 'I didn't mean it to sound horrid, but she just turned round and said, "Fuck off." I was trying to compliment her, but she thought I was being bitchy. I went to say goodbye to her when I left but she wouldn't talk to me and we didn't talk for three months. I sent her a card saying I was sorry and I tried ringing her but she put the phone down, so I left messages. In the end she believed me, but we're not as close as we were. I now know that I have to be careful what I say to her and that doesn't make friendship easy.' If Sally had simply replied, 'Thanks Susie, did I really look that bad?' Or 'Wow! Do you know how to make a friend feel good', the accidental slight would have been batted back, apologies made and accepted and three months of wasted righteous indignation and guilt could have been avoided.

Women can be really bad at confronting their friends when they say or do something to piss them off. We would rather not turn something small into an issue and risk losing that friend completely, just like teenage girls. It's a habit that can be hard to bust. We know it's better to just let it pass, but like elephants we find it hard to forget, and fester. One woman emailed me to tell me how a friend had said to her mother in the 1970s, 'You're the sort of woman who would take her children to a football match and not let them scream.' 'It was so untrue but my mother never forgot it. When she was in hospital dying of cancer, this "good woman" did her duty by visiting, but my mother got so angry I had to make some excuse to get the woman to leave.' We have to let off steam somewhere, so we foster duplicity, discussing their motives with mutual friends rather than simply telling them straight. The novelist Elizabeth Noble compares it to playing chess, 'Bitching goes hand in hand with close friendship because not all of your friends please you at the same time. You have to remember what you've said to whom and not all friends can be trusted.'

We pride ourselves as amateur psychotherapists, unravelling the motives and genetic influences of family and friends with those we are close to and often those interpretations are enlightening. We take pride in our intuition, or psychological insights, and we seek out those insights in our women friends and often those discussions become couched in empathetic tones – 'I think she must have a really hard time with that son of hers . . .' (he's autistic/on drugs/failing at school/gay) – and the simple question 'How's X?' will illicit much more of an answer than 'fine'. We love to talk about the nitty-gritty of each other's lives. Intimate discussions with others help us to be more understanding and forgiving of friends who are in emotional difficulties or who offend us. When friends confide in us, we are often not as honest as we could be. We don't want to risk causing offence or being wrong. How do you tell a close friend whose marriage is in difficulties that it's probably over because you know he is having an affair with somebody and that he once made a pass at you? You don't. But you might well need to tell another mutual friend that.

'Women may not be two-faced when they agree with an inter-locutor and then criticise them when they are no longer present,' explains linguist Jennifer Coates. 'They are simply maximising the common ground between them while expressing their own feelings.' But if you know that you are in some veiled sense put-ting that other person down, and elevating yourself in the process, then you might need to take a long hard look inside yourself rather than at others. Why does this issue matter to you so much and why do you want to be that much closer to this par-ticular woman? There's nothing wrong with wanting to forge more intimate friendships with others, but friendship grows because of the support and loyalty you offer. When you exchange intimacies with another you render yourself vulnerable. Women know each other so well that they also know where to hit so that it really hurts if they want to. 'When one woman takes aim at the heart of another, she rarely fails to find the vulnerable spot and the wound she inflicts is incurable,' says Madame De Merteuil in *Les Liaisons Dangereuses*. Few want to risk forging close friend-ships with those who might betray their trust.

Just like teenagers, women tend to bitch about the aspects of their lives they feel most insecure about. Stylish image, youth and beauty still mean so much more for cultural and social acceptance for women than they do for men. Adult bitch code over appearance is complex. 'You're looking well' from someone with bitching intent can mean 'You've put on weight,' and 'You've lost weight' can mean 'You looked really fat last week.' One of the ultimate style put-downs came from the actress and queen bitch of Hollywood, Joan Crawford, who walked up to Ingrid Bergman, whom she had never liked, and said: 'Ingrid darling, I simply *adore* your dress. Tell me, did you make it yourself?' I've been told of one woman who chose to anthropomorphise a fat cat to make their point – 'Presumably he's on the same diet as the rest of the family.' Age is also often a sore point, 'I'm never quite sure what friends mean when they say "Oh Virginia, when you get to our age . . ." says Virginia Ironside. 'You can't exactly say "Shut up, don't be so rude."'

Motherhood is another area of life where women feel deeply insecure and therefore competitive. We need each other that much more for advice and support as mothers but because we feel so uncertain at times as to whether we're doing it right or indeed are any good at it, we're often a little too quick to put others down. Mothers like to divide themselves into camps as a way of distinguishing themselves within a large amorphous group, just as teenagers do, and the media enflames these divisions by calling them things like the 'Mummy Wars'. We're breast- or bottle-feeders, working or stay at home mothers, liberal or disciplined parents, and by reassuring ourselves that they are doing the right thing, through association with a particular camp, we feel they have licence to attack others for doing it differently. I remember being profoundly shocked interviewing new mothers for my book *Life After Birth* by the way that one woman declared that she could never be friends with a woman who bottle-fed her baby. She felt it necessary to denounce every other woman who chose bottle-feeding in order to shore up her decision to chain herself to regular feeds as well as the agony of mastisis simply because it was better for her own baby. She was being the 'Good' mother. But what if that bottle-feeder she had to despise couldn't feed her own baby for some reason and wanted to? What if that bottle-feeder turned out to be a lifelong salvation and laugh of a friend?

When mothers lack a sure sense of self, it's not enough to just be the mothers they are, good in some respects, crap in others, because women feel permanently on trial as mothers, a trial they can never win. 'I've met some lovely mums but I would have to say that the majority have been overly critical of any parenting technique not validated by themselves. I do a number of classes with my pre-school children. I constantly have to listen to comments like "I don't see the point of spend-ing endless amounts of money on classes, the park's good enough," but what I chose to do for my children is my business as is how I spend my money,' said one mother on the 'Mumsnet' chatroom (www.mumsnet.com). Another mother on the same thread said a woman had recently asked, 'Are your children really bright or are schools just too easy to get into these days?' It takes a rock-solid sense that one is doing the right thing to be able to bat off these comments and not take them to heart.

When we invite women friends into our homes our house-wifery skills and home assets are also up for inspection. When we join a book club our intellectual capabilities are on show. As with all the best gangs in school, joining a reading group can be difficult. You have to be invited to join a select group of women or else form your own. In the US, some book clubs have waiting lists and conduct interviews and one group even asked a member to leave because she hadn't been to a university. Your CV of reading is on display ('You mean you haven't read *Middlemarch*?!' in shock horror) as well as your wallpaper, and it's only with the cosiest group of friends (like those in my book group) that you can admit that you didn't understand the end or found it so hardgoing that you skipped the entire middle section. When it comes to suggesting the next book that can also be tricky. What am I saying about myself if I suggest Joanna Trollope rather than Plato? When the novelist Rachel Cusk moved to Bristol she joined a book group, a group of women who 'processed the steady stream of contemporary literature with the application of an all-female decoding centre appointed by a cultural minister of war.' When she found herself defending Chekhov's brilliance one evening and then received an email saying that book group was getting far too serious, she resigned and wrote a damning piece about this particular book group and its attitude to literature in the *Guardian* on 28 August 2005. Charlotte Hooper, another member of the book group, retaliated with a letter in the *Guardian* the following Saturday: 'When writer Rachel Cusk asked to join our book group we welcomed her as a fellow reader and local mother. In retrospect this was a mistake', Hooper went on to say how their modest aim was to read a novel a month in a non-judgemental atmosphere, but Cusk was unable to forget the day job, determined to impose her own lofty views . . . she cast far more gloom than Chekhov ever managed and precipitated a rash of resignations.

The cars we drive, whether we shop at Tesco or Waitrose and designer label clothes help us to identify and bond with other people of like mind. We're no different to teenagers in that respect, and the more insecure we feel, the more these seemingly fixed points of status seem to matter and get put down in others. We preface bitching with statements like 'She's one of my closest friends/I'm deeply fond of her but . . . have you seen the size of her new kitchen? We bitch about women who appear to have so much more than we do because we want those things. We slag off other women who seem to be able to juggle six immaculately dressed and well-behaved children with a full-time high-flying job. If we acknowledge that these are statements born simply of our own envy and add that slice of humour (*and* she's got great legs, bitch!) we maintain confidence and intimacy. No one else ever needs to know.

'Gossip has been argued variously to disseminate information, entertain, establish norms, exercise social control, enhance in-group bonding,' writes psychologist Anne Campbell in her paper 'Female Competition: Causes, Constraints, Content and Contexts'. 'But it is also a potent form of indirect competition. When we gossip about another person we simultaneously achieve two goals. Most obviously we spread information that is damaging to the other's reputation and so diminish his or her social standing. But the act of condemnation is also an act of self-promotion; one cannot credibly accuse a rival of behaviours that one engages in oneself.' Over time we learn to navigate the difference between benign and destructive gossip, we recognise patterns of behaviour that we do not trust because of past betrayals and we get better at interpreting bitch code and the hidden motives of women. Most of the time we gossip to bond and bitch to let off steam. Most of the time that works and we maintain life-long relationships. But perhaps those relationships could be even stronger and closer if women could find the strength to talk about things honestly and openly. As we grow older, we learn to value friendship between women for its lasting sense of support and mutual respect, something that can be hard to find from any other source. We trust that our true friends will not betray us and we learn not to form close and confiding relationships with those who bitch to such an extent about others that there is no doubt that they are putting us down too.

If I see that woman again I'm going to pull out every hair on her chin.

Tallulah Bankhead

'Boys and Girls'
by Michele Hanson

My friend Clayden met Gardener out and about the other day. Naturally they said not a word about our ex-relationship or the state of play in anyone's personal life. They may have mentioned Iraq. Then Clayden met another chap he has known for decades. No mention of personal relationships or women. They sat more or less silently together on the train for fifteen minutes. Not the tiniest smidgin of gossip or scandal passed their lips. Then in came news of another sighting of Gardener. My old friend Toad had spotted him in the street. Again, no detailed report was forthcoming.

Had one of these sightings been by a woman, I would have expected a fairly thorough inquisition to have taken place, and then to have received a detailed report back, 'He was doing so-and-so and he said blah-blah-blah and he looked like: (precise description given of physical state, outfit, demeanour, mood, and degree of function or suffering).' Naturally I interrogated Clayden and Toad but discovered only an information desert. Q: How was he? A: All right/Very well. Q: What did he say? A: Nothing much.

Meanwhile, Rosemary visited her friend's nephew in Argentina. Her father had had an affair with this chap's grandmother, her sister had been engaged to his father and naturally Rosemary was busting for details. But Nephew's lips were sealed. If only it had been a niece.

Now compare and contrast. I suddenly hear from one of the exes of one of my exes. She provides thrilling details of their relationship and in-depth analyses of this fellow's behaviour which support my theories and mirror my experience. This sort of cross-checking can be a great comfort. You may wonder why you ever liked this fellow. The years of dreadfulness may have blotted out the heavenly bits, or perhaps there were no heavenly bits but you were blinded by lust and thought there were. Information exchange can clear up these grey areas and show that you are not alone in your poor judgment/ inability to form delightful relationships/ desire for information.

However do men manage without this facility? According to Fielding, they are too noble to indulge in gossip. It is beneath them. 'We are deep,' he brags, citing Donne, Keats and Fotherington-Thomas. 'We have feelings too. We just don't gas about them interminably.'

But what might those feelings be? We want to know. 'Er . . .'

Pride and Prejudice
by Jane Austen
(Elizabeth to Jane)

'Oh! You are a great deal too apt, you know to like people in general. You never see a fault in anybody. All the world are good and agreeable in your eyes. I have never heard you speak ill of a human being in your life.'

'I would not wish to be hasty in censuring anyone; but I always speak what I think.'

'I know you do; and it is *that* which makes the wonder. With *your* good sense, to be so honestly blind to the follies and nonsense of others! Affectation of candour is common enough; – One meets it everywhere. But to be candid without ostentation or design – to take the good of everybody's character and make it still better, and say nothing of the bad – belongs to you alone.'

Hell Hath No Fury Like a Woman Scorned

In general, I think women should be each other's human wonderbras – uplifting, supportive and making each other look bigger and better . . . But once crossed, you know, if you find she's sleeping with your husband, I do know how to be a bionic bitch.

1) Turn her bathroom scales up by half a stone
2) Put Nair hair remover in her mascara wand
3) Smear tiger balm in her panty liners
4) Tell her it's a fancy dress party when its not, meaning you'll arrive wearing a chic little black number and she'll be dressed as a garden gnome with a sausage on a string.
5) Become the Navratilova of the back-handed compliment. Practise your put-down beforehand. Something like 'I wish men would appreciate me for my brain instead of my breasts. I wish I could make myself less attractive. So, tell me, how do YOU do it?'

Kathy Lette

I swear . . . If you existed, I'd divorce you.
Martha in *Who's Afraid of Virginia Woolf?*
by Edward Albee

The full quote from William Congreve's play *The Mourning Bride* is 'Heaven has no rage like love to hatred turned/ nor hell a fury like a woman scorned' and it's a poignant one. If you believe what the evolutionary psychologists have to say about sex and the primary urge to reproduce, women bitch more with each other as they fight for the favours of men than they do over anything else. Women have less time to reproduce, they need to invest heavily in their offspring to maximise their child's chances of survival and success and they have less choice when it comes to finding a good father for their children.

Is it all down to biology or do basic gender inequalities effect our behaviour? The jury's still out on evolutionary psychology versus socialisation of genders. However, men primarily use status and wealth to attract a mate, for women need financial and practical support to raise their offspring to maturity successfully. Men compete with each other for the most attractive (fertile) women with intellectual or sports prowess and the more obvious displays of status. 'Males are competing for status and resources which are associated with the prize of fathering a disproportionate number of children,' writes psychologist Anne Campbell in her paper 'Female Competition: Causes, Constraints, Content and Contexts'. 'And because males are willing to inseminate women promiscuously (where little or no paternal care is required of them) women have no need to compete for copulations.' But they do need to compete with each other for economic and practical support, for 'resources which can be converted to offspring and so enhance their reproductive success'. We compete through our appearance to be noticed, flaunting our assets to attract a man. We smile and flirt at men because it pays to do so. Men approach women who flirt more than even the most attractive woman who does-n't. And flirting gives us valuable information, 'that inviting look, followed by coyness, imitates an approach–withdraw sequence found in most mammalian species where survival of newborns requires a father's help, and so the female needs to test a male's willingness to pursue and commit,' writes Daniel Goleman in his book *Social Intelligence*. Raising children to maturity is a difficult job to do alone, so women compete with each other for those few good, lucrative men in the areas they know that men value the most – looks, youth and physical attractiveness (which signify fertility to a male), as well as fidelity and sexual reputation (which matters to a man because it helps to guarantee that the child he invests in is actually his). It is no coincidence that appearance and sexual reputa-tion are the two most common topics for bitching amongst adolescent girls, when sexual hormones first surface.

Aggression in both sexes is at its height between the ages of fifteen and twenty-four when young people need to establish themselves in the mating game. Both sexes experience similar levels of aggression, but generally they express that aggression in different ways. Men use physical aggression as a means of asserting dominance and status as well as acquiring resources. It tends to be men who engage in more violent and risky crime, men who drive faster and men who have more accidents both at home and on the streets. Women tend to be less keen on taking risks generally. 'One way women can compete without risking their safety or compromising their lives is through acts that ostracise, stigmatise, and otherwise exclude others from social interaction without risking direct confrontation,' writes Anne Campbell. 'Such acts do not eliminate or physically injure the target, nor do they demonstrate the greater size, strength or belligerence of the attacker. They do, however, inflict stress and diminish the opponent's reputation and social support. Women don't seem to put each other down for being poor. They are far more likely to accuse others of being fat, lazy, a bad mother or a bit of a slag.'

Women are capable of unwittingly undermining each other in the sexual arena in highly subtle and complex ways. A small study of fifty-seven female and forty-seven male university students at York University in Toronto, Canada found that women were far more critical of each other's appearance during their most fertile periods (day 12 to day 21 of their cycle) than they were of women when their oestrogen levels were lower (*New Scientist*, 18/2/2004). Maryann Fisher, author of the study, says, 'When you're in a high fertility phase you have to be more able to judge other women as potential rivals. Rather than saying "I'm going to beat that woman up because she looked at you," it's "Oh my goodness, look how fat her ankles are." Does putting someone down make you feel better about yourself? Or does saying it to a male make her less attractive to him?' Both. It's a clever tactic and we're not the only female species to use it.

Primatologists such as S.B. Hrdy and Barbara Smuts have noted that females of many species such as gorillas, baboons, marmosets and tamarins disrupt each other's reproductive cycles. 'Females have been observed to engage in sustained, low-level harassment of other females,' writes Anne Campbell in 'Female Competition'. 'The target is consistently interrupted and displaced as she tries to rest, feed or mate. The resulting stress suppresses oestrus and can cause abortion, diminishing the reproductive success of the victim.' Female wolves read each other's hormone balance all the time and alpha wolves will engage in relentless bullying of subordinate female wolves if they smell fertile and appear to want to compete for her position as chief fertile female. She keeps the subordinate female in her place, mouthing to encourage her to roll over and submit, or, if that fails, with snapping, snarling and biting. The primatologist Carole Jahme writes in her book *Beauty and the Beasts* of how some female primates harass and eject their own daughters if they become sexually mature and therefore breeding competitors when they are still fertile themselves. 'All animals need to compete when resources are scarce and that includes women,' writes Anne Campbell. As the resources get scarcer in poorer areas with high unemployment, levels of physical aggression rise. 'Women can and do use physical aggression where the competition for reproductively relevant resources becomes extreme.'

Anne Campbell concludes in her paper 'Female Competition' that the vast cultural change of the past fifty years with feminism and greater equality between the sexes has not fundamentally altered the nature of female competition. But perhaps that shift has already started. Research conducted by Fhionna Moore at the University of St Andrews in 2006 on 1851 women between the ages of eighteen and thirty-five, found that financially independent women seem to be looking more now for good looks in a man rather than financial security, while women with less control over their cash still rated a man's financial status more (*New Scientist* 6/4/2006). Greater emphasis on male style and grooming could also be a consequence of greater economic independence amongst women – shape up boys if you want to spread that seed. However long it takes, one fact is incontrovertible: We may be driven by our biology and the reproductive imperative in more ways than we realise, but we are also the only species with the intellect to rise above it.

Great Bitch Revenge Stories

Once women are in established relationships with children they can be even more vulnerable. It is middle-aged men who tend to leave their family for younger women. When it happens, the abandoned woman feels doubly betrayed. Not only has she lost much of the support she needs to bring up her children (four out of five absent fathers pay nothing towards the upkeep of their children according to the Child Support Agency) but she also feels, as a mother and older woman, that she has limited opportunities to form a loving relationship with another man. She has every reason to get very cross indeed. So the rage inherent to being dumped erupts in other imaginative ways. I've been told of ex-wives who have cut up their husband's suits, of an ex-wife who circled the church where her former husband was getting remarried shouting, 'You bastard' to the assembled guests out of the window of her car. Another packed up all her husband's possessions and had them delivered to the restaurant where her husband was having a business lunch. Other imaginative acts of revenge include the wife who found a condom in her husband's jacket pocket when she was taking it to the dry cleaners. She had been sterilised after her third child. So she took the jacket to the cleaners, stabbed the condom repeatedly with a pin and then put it back. One wronged wife got so angry she took the golden retriever to the vet, had him castrated and when her husband came to 'collect his things' he found the dog tied to the banisters in the hall with a label around his neck saying 'you're next'. Then there's the woman who sent a recorded delivery packet to her husband's female boss and put the words 'Erectile Dysfunctional Association' in the slot marked 'sender' . . .

I had a 'friend', who I subsequently discovered was having an affair with my husband, who found every possible way to put me down. When I decorated a room she said 'I like your wallpaper, did you make it yourself?' When we were discussing what colours we thought people were once I said I thought she was emerald green. She said 'Lucy, when I think of you I think of beige.'

One ex-wife rung up her ex-husband's new bride two days before their wedding, ostensibly to speak to her son, who wasn't there. 'She explained carefully to me that their son didn't want to be at our wedding, that the marriage mattered to me, but that it didn't matter to anyone else. I wasn't the catalyst for their break-up, she left him way before he met me, so I should have retaliated but I didn't, I went off and cried instead. I subsequently discovered that she had told everyone at their son's school that her husband had left her for me, alienating us at school. James couldn't understand why everyone was being so cold to him. Then at her son's 21st birthday party she sat me on a table of rugger buggers. Weddings bring out the worst in people.'

A couple from Wandsworth were on a shooting party in Scotland, where a 'friend' told the wife that her husband was shagging the hostess. So she 'accidentally' filled his behind with buckshot after she 'tripped' over a clump of heather and he had to be taken into A and E to have the pellets picked out of his scrotum. She gave him a bottle of malt whisky when she went in to visit him with a 'get well' card that said, 'Hope this puts some more lead in your pencil.'

I was visiting my aunt a few years ago. She didn't get on very well with her husband, a policeman. One morning he was shouting at her, complaining that the packed lunches she made for him to take to work were never very nice. When he went to the bathroom, my aunt took the ham sandwiches she'd been making for him, opened them up carefully and bent down to let the dog lick the ham before re-closing the sandwiches and packing them in the lunchbox. She smiled all the while. They're now divorced.

Jerry Hall couldn't resist having a dig at her ex Mick Jagger at a fashion awards night in Monte Carlo in October 2005. When she was asked by co-host Jeremy Irons whether Mick might host the event with her next year she said, 'Are you insane? Have you seen how many models there are here? Even he couldn't afford the child support payments.' Then when she was asked whether she would be doing any betting during her stay, she said she wouldn't, but that she liked the odd flutter on horses. Then she said, 'Of course Mick always liked betting on a lot of fillies at the same time. Unfortunately the last filly he bet on, I got to keep the house.' (*Daily Mail*, 19/10/2005)

Hah! I always knew Frank would end up in bed with a boy.

Ava Gardner on Sinatra's marriage to Mia Farrow.

~

I look on my friendship with her as like having a gall-stone. You deal with it, there is pain, and then you pass it. That's all I have to say about Schmadonna.

Sandra Bernhard

~

She's just a bossy old bag. If he had not died the marriage would not have lasted. They had some terrible fights. Bogie didn't give a damn. He was a great man and I loved him madly. I was the only person, man or woman, who could match him drink for drink. I am Bacall's worst nightmare.

Verity Thompson, wig-maker who met Humphrey Bogart in 1942 when he was forty-three and practically bald. She was twenty-three.
***(The Week*, 27/8/2005)**

Ulrika Johnson on Nancy Dell'Olio after her four-month affair with Sven Goran Eriksson. 'In a way, I think I've done her a world of good. She is incredibly well known now and that's something she obviously enjoys,' she told *Hello* magazine. When Nancy compared herself to Yoko Ono, Johnson wrote in her *News of the World* column, 'Is that because neither you nor Yoko is over 3ft? Or just that without your Eriksson you'd be absolutely nothing and no one?'

'Go fuck yourself, Pyrah'
'That's the best offer you've made me so far.'

dumped boyfriend to Gill Pyrah

~

I thought I told you to wait in the car.

Tallulah Bankhead on seeing a former lover for the first time in years

JULIE and SUSAN are on their way to Mary Alice's funeral.

JULIE: Mom, why would someone kill themselves?

SUSAN: Well, sometimes people are so unhappy, they think that's the only way they can solve their problems.

JULIE: But Mrs Young always seemed happy.

SUSAN: Yeah, but sometimes people pretend to be one way on the outside, when they're totally different on the inside.

JULIE: Oh, you mean like how Dad's girlfriend is always smiling and saying nice things, but deep down, you just know she's a bitch?

SUSAN: I don't like that word Julie, but yeah, that's a great example.

Desperate Housewives

Age doesn't matter to him and size doesn't matter to her.

Brittany Murphy, ex-girlfriend of Ashton Kutcher when he started dating Demi Moore

There was this young woman who was after all/any of our men. She was hanging around in the pub one night and a female friend of mine decided to embarrass her away. So she stared at her relentlessly, up and down her body, up and down. Eventually the woman asked if she could help her. 'Yes, you can,' my friend replied. 'Your price tag appears to have fallen off.' It worked.

email from Deirdre in Wolverhampton

And maybe revenge isn't the most effective strategy . . .

> The best revenge sometimes is not to cut up the suits or to pour the claret down the sink, but to not let the other side have its resolution, to refuse to engage and go as they want you to go. They want you to scream and shout and say 'Stay, stay with me' but if you just go off and do your own thing they really don't like that. The other thing is to live well and not be invisible, show them how well you are without them but maintain a sense of grace and integrity. Find that grace to recast your life and do it well.
>
> Elizabeth Buchan, author of *Revenge of the Middle Age Woman*

> The average man is more interested in a woman who is interested in him than he is in a woman with beautiful legs
>
> Marlene Dietrich

Bitch
Carolyn Kizer

Now, when he and I meet, after all these years,
I say to the bitch inside me, don't start growling.
He isn't a trespasser anymore,
just an old acquaintance tipping his hat.
My voice says, 'Nice to see you,'

As the bitch starts to bark hysterically.
He isn't an enemy now,
Where are your manners, I say as I say,
'How are the children? They must be growing up.'
At a kind word from him, a look like the old days,
The bitch changes her tone: she begins to whimper.
She wants to snuggle up to him, to cringe.
Down, girl! Keep your distance
Or I'll give you a taste of the choke-chain.
'Fine, I'm just fine,' I tell him.
She slobbers and grovels.
After all, I am her mistress. She is basically loyal.
It's just that she remembers how she came running
Each evening, when she heard his step;
How she lay at his feet and looked up adoringly
Though he was absorbed in his paper;
Or, bored with her devotion, ordered her to the kitchen
Until he was ready to play.
But the small careless kindnesses
When he'd had a good day, or a couple of drinks,
Come back to her now, seem more important
Than the casual cruelties, the ultimate dismissal.
'It's nice to see you doing so well,' I say.
He couldn't have taken you with him;
You were too demonstrative, too clumsy,
Not like the well groomed pets of his new friends.
'Give my regards to your wife,' I say. You gag
As I drag you off by the scruff,
Saying, 'Goodbye! Goodbye! Nice to see you again.'

Sisters Are Doin' It For Themselves

Why, Sir, I trust I may have leave to speak;
And speak I will. I am no child, no babe.
Your betters have endur'd me say my mind
And if you cannot, best you stop your ears.
My tongue will tell the anger of my heart,
Or else my heart, concealing it, will break;
And rather than it shall, I will be free
Even to the uttermost, as I please, in words.

Katherine to Petruchio, Act 4 Scene 3
The Taming of the Shrew **by William Shakespeare**

For the first time in history women can define themselves by their careers and by what they do in the wider world rather than just as somebody's wife or mother. Girls grow up with greater ambitions and expectations. They want more for themselves – good jobs, money, freedom to do what they please and they expect more from their men as lovers, partners and fathers. Feminism has improved life and relationships for men and women in countless ways. However, so much of our sense of self is still constrained by stereotypical notions of how each sex should behave. Men are expected to be strong, forceful, courageous and allowed to be

dominant and egotistical; women are considered more affectionate, empathetic, sensitive and emotional. They nurture
others for the common good, as part of a team rather than as
ambitious individuals. Age-old stereotypes, that women are
either self-sacrificing, maternal saints or ball-breaking
whores, have not gone away.

There is far more that unites us as human beings than
divides us as men and women – we're all capable of anger, jealousy, selfishness, envy, aggression and even violence – but
mercifully, we also all share an even greater propensity for
compassion, kindness, consideration of others, love and the
need to help or nurture those we care about who find themselves in greater need – yet we love to focus on the differences
between the sexes. We're fascinated by them within our families, friends and marriages, and in the media. Girls are still
typecast as 'good' (Jennifer Aniston, Kylie) or 'bad' (Angelina
Jolie, Christina Aguilera). Strong-minded girls with an opinion (like Hermione in Harry Potter) are put down as 'bossy'
(fledgling bitch), while a similarly bossy boy would be considered authoritative and a natural leader. Catfights between
women make good drama, 'Female rivalries thrill in a way that
disputes between men don't. When you write about two
women arguing you can really go for it,' says Paul Marquess,
executive producer on *The Bill* and *Family Affairs*. 'Men are
much more buttoned up and resort to violence much quicker,
so women having an altercation lend themselves more readily
to drama. Women are supposed to behave themselves, so the
transgression of them misbehaving is more exciting than it
would be if it were two men fighting.' (*Guardian* 15/4/2004)

The more macho skills of competitive drive and

Machiavellian ruthlessness essential for success in the work-place often sit uneasily with the more 'feminine' side and the false construct that we should always support other women just because they are women. 'The women's movement gave us licence to enter environments in which ambition, power and authority reigned,' writes Nan Mooney in her book *I Can't Believe She Did That*. 'Sisterhood left us little context to discuss the conflicts these environments would inevitably create among women on the job.' If we persist with the self-sacrificing, kind and 'good' girl within working environments, people tend to misunderstand, take advantage and walk all over us. But if we then also strive like one of the boys, to get ahead, we're somehow alienated from other women. We still lack enough role models. 'Female' and 'Power' are still rela-tively new partners and we're not quite sure yet what that looks like when it's normal. And sometimes I think that we are our own worst enemies, partly because we want it all – home and work – and partly because we're still so uncertain of our position in society as powerful economically independent women, that we're clinging onto the rest of our perceived char-acter assets. We sell ourselves short by assuming that we cannot achieve something because the odds are still so stacked against us and because we try to do too much.

We know that a sense of home really matters and want to keep control over it, from deciding how to decorate a room, to shopping and cooking, to assuming the lion's share of the childcare. Yes I know that men are often reluctant to do the cleaning or the nappy-changing, but how often is that because we're not prepared to make them do it because we don't want to give up that sense of female identity that is so linked to

home and children? We maintain unrealistic expectations of
other women. We expect them always to be kind, never cruel;
and then when they put themselves first, we cry – selfish
bitches. We expect our close female friends to step into maternal roles, supporting us when we are needy. When they don't
or can't it's a betrayal. We hold our own mothers to the
unachievable 'Good Mother' paradigm and blame them for all
the things they didn't do for us. And we blame ourselves for
not being the perfect mothers we feel we should be, for working instead of constantly being at home, for buying birthday
cakes instead of making them ourselves, for failing to engage
with Play-Doh or playgrounds because we find them boring.
And, we still want to be thought of as attractive and sexy!

If we could give up unrealistic expectations of other women
we would make it easier for ourselves as woman. We're allowed
to be competitive, ambitious, ruthless and calculating in pur-
suit of our dreams and success. That doesn't negate kindness
and respect for others. We can be less self-sacrificing and be
better mothers as a result, simply because we show our children
that women are not doormats and can be happier in life. We
can decide to be happy enough with the way we look and focus
on the strengths and assets that we have rather than allowing
envy of what others have to devour us. And we're allowed to
get really angry, rip-roaringly angry, when things go wrong.

Competitive and collaborative instincts are not necessarily
direct opposites. If we let our fear of failure or of not being
liked stand in the way of our individual ambition, we run the
risk of selling ourselves short and downplaying our genuine
expertise. If we don't put ourselves first and compete for what
we want from life, we run the risk of being overly competitive

for our children in order to compensate for our own disappointments, which is not in their best interests. We're not being selfish or unfeminine by pursuing our ambitions with gusto. With less to resent about our own lives, there's also less to resent in others. If we don't sell ourselves short, we're less likely to feel the need to judge others or to put them down by being the bitch. The confidence that comes from achieving just *some* of our goals can also give women greater confidence in one of the areas we find most difficult – being more forgiving of each other's weaknesses and finding ways to be more honest and openly critical with other women when they've offended us badly. When we have proper conversations expressing hurt, anger and regret, directly to one another, the boil ready to bust with bitching is lanced and relations are usually closer. Otherwise we trigger the same biological shifts that accompanied the original encounter, that same lethal cocktail of raised blood pressure and unresolved rage.

The longer we allow things to fester the worse they tend to get and the bitchier we become. Anne Robinson accused Lynda La Plante of lying about her age in a newspaper column in 2003. Lynda La Plante was trying to adopt a child at the time and was deeply worried that these accusations would reduce her chances of succeeding. 'The remarks triggered a total invasion of my privacy and some unbearably nasty vitriol about me in the media. It was the most stressful time in my life,' says La Plante. *Two years later* La Plante was having lunch at The Ivy, spotted Anne Robinson across the room and felt angry all over again. She discussed ordering Spaghetti Bolognese and tossing it over Robinson's head with her friend, but they quickly dismissed that idea. Instead, she went over to

Robinson's table and according to fellow Ivy diner Ivan Massow (*Daily Mail*, 8/11/2005), said, 'Hello, my name is Lynda La Plante and you destroyed my life for a year.' 'This isn't the time or the place,' replied Anne Robinson. 'Nor was a newspaper column with two million readers,' said La Plante before returning to her table. 'Everyone should confront things, and behave decently,' said La Plante afterwards. But one can't help wondering why she didn't confront Robinson properly in the first instance.

Women tend to pick on each other because they cannot rage effectively against the wider injustices they face as women. Dismantling the stereotypes that keep us in our place is the most effective start and we can all do that as individuals. We don't have to be 'good' or 'perfect', selfless and constantly compassionate. If we rid ourselves of the stereotypical notions compromising women with models of goodness, which they don't feel comfortable with, we also rid ourselves of the 'bad girl' bitch stereotype, which can at times of stress and great insecurity feel like our only means of expression and escape. As women grow older they have a tendency to lose inhibition and care less what others think of them. When you're released from the mating game and the reproductive imperative, appearance and pleasing others matters less than pleasing yourself. If we could adopt that same confidence, that same sureness of self at a much earlier age, how much more could we all achieve, personally as well as politically . . . I wonder . . .

It's still such early days, true equality of opportunity continues to elude us and women have to navigate and juggle the worlds of work and home as best they can. It's all so exhausting trying to do both perfectly, it's a wonder that we're not harridans and bitches all of the time! It may be too late for my generation raised on the idealistic hope of being able to 'have it all' and 'be it all', but it isn't too late for our daughters. If we encourage healthy expression of ambition and competition through sports and debates when they are young, they will be better equipped to stand up for themselves, confront others honestly and diplomatically and compete more effectively as adults. With a firmer sense of themselves as distinct and powerful individuals, they will feel the need to bitch or denigrate other women less.

> **Women who seek equality with men are not setting their standards very high.**
>
> **Fridge magnet**

Feminist Spats

Feminists are often grand mistresses of the art of bitchery. Their public spats are hugely entertaining because they can be so horribly rude to one another, but their chutzpah should also be celebrated. We need these women in our lives. They're braver because they are not constrained by conventional notions of manners and how women should behave. They're beyond caring what others think of them and are not afraid of the consequences when they say what they think. There's very little innuendo to their bitchery – these 'bad girls' go straight for the jugular . . . and that's thrilling and hugely enjoyable for the rest of us who could never quite dare to be this honest . . .

~

When Mary McCarthy met Susan Sontag in the late 1960s, McCarthy said, 'Oh, you're the imitation me.' Thirty years later when Camille Paglia met Sontag she expected to be acknowledged in the same way, to be handed on the baton, but Sontag said nothing. 'I wanted to say "I'm your successor, dammit, and you don't have the wit to realise it",' said Paglia. When Paglia's *Sexual Personae* appeared in 1990, Paglia got her revenge on

Sontag. 'I've been chasing that bitch for twenty-five years,' she told *Vanity Fair* magazine, 'and I've finally passed her! She could scarcely retain her intellectual preeminence while not having heard of a controversial woman thinker of my prominence.'

Elaine Showalter – *Inventing Herself: Claiming a Feminist Intellectual Heritage*

Julie Burchill on Germaine Greer's appearance on *Big Brother*:

When I was a wide-eyed 12-year-old teenybopper, I shoplifted *The Female Eunuch* and thought this must be the cleverest, wittiest, most compassionate woman in the world . . . Now she appears to be the sort of rancid bore who one would actually leave a quite lively party to avoid being cornered by. She genuinely has lost some of her marvellous marbles and, like an old lady lifting up her dress and revealing her genitalia to a weeping world, simply does not understand how loony she looks. The other, which is even sadder, is that this woman, who once seemed blessed with the world's biggest BS detector, has spent so long amongst the arrogant autistics of academia that she has lost much of the common sense that the Australian people are as a rule so rich in.

The Times, 13/1/2005

When columnist Suzanne Moore accused Greer of having had a hysterectomy, Greer hit back with a vitriolic attack on her appearance. 'So much lipstick must rot the brain . . . Hair bird's-nested all over the place, fuck-me shoes and three fat layers of cleavage.'

Camille Paglia once called Naomi Wolf 'The Dan Quayle of feminism, a pretty airhead who has gotten any profile whatsoever because of her hair'; 'A *Seventeen* magazine level of thinker'; and 'Little Miss Pravda'. Then in 2004 when Wolf wrote a cover story for *New York* magazine in which she alleged that her professor Harold Bloom (also Paglia's professor) had sexually harassed her by putting his hand on her thigh – Paglia let rip again. 'It really grates on me that Naomi Wolf for her entire life has been batting her eyes and bobbing her boobs in the face of men and made a profession out of courting male attention by flirting and offering sexual allure.'

Guardian, 20/2/04

Julie Burchill trashed Paglia's book *Sexual Personae* in a review for the *Spectator* magazine. Toby Young, editor of the *Modern Review* then asked Paglia to review Burchill's novel *No Exit* and 'Rip her to shreds'. Paglia refused. When Toby Young asked if he could publish her fax in the *Modern Review*, Paglia took the story straight to the *Sunday Times*.

The following fax exchange between Burchill and Paglia
took place in March 1993:

Burchill to Paglia:

I'm surprised you were upset by my *Spectator* review. How
you of all people can complain of my 'malice' is a
complete mystery to me. Now you know how Naomi Wolf
and Susan Faludi must feel every time you spew up your
spiel to a waiting world . . . I know ethnicity means a lot
to you. You've got a wop name so you think you're Robert
De Niro. These little girls, Jewish and middle-class and
whatever, are too nice, too well bred to fight back. I'm
not . . . I'm not as loud as you, but if push comes to shove
I'm nastier. I'm ten years younger, two stone heavier, and I
haven't had my nuts taken off by academia.

Paglia to Burchill:

What empty bluster and tired clichés! If you were once
witty, I'm afraid you're in a bit of a decline. I have no idea
who you are. Your review of my book was not particularly
negative . . . your weaknesses and limitations as a thinker
and writer were very much on view in it . . . I am read and
translated around the world from Japan to South America,
and the basis of my fame is not just journalism but a
scholarly book on the history of culture. You are a very
local commodity, completely unknown outside of England,
and you have produced nothing of global interest . . . your
coarse and unskilled letter is yet another way you have
wounded yourself and I will make sure it is widely seen.

Burchill to Paglia:

It's great to see an academic cube like yourself get with it. I'm very glad you're big in Japan . . .

Paglia to Burchill:

Your spluttering hostility proves I have made serious inroads into territory you once ruled alone. It is hard to believe you are a woman in your mid-thirties. Your flip clichéd locutions, braying rhetoric, and meandering incoherences are those of a college or even high school student . . . You think yourself madly clever, but I'm afraid your *enfant terrible* personality is a bit tattered. You seem trapped in juvenility . . .

Burchill to Paglia:

Dear Professor Paglia,

Fuck off you crazy old dyke.

Always,

Julie Burchill

For the full text see 'Fax off and Die, Bitch!' on www.julieburchill.org.uk

Camille Paglia is simply a media creation. Perhaps she exists, but whether or not she exists doesn't matter – she is just a media fantasy, a nobody. She just mouths. She is just a screeching female character who attacks other women and calls herself a feminist.

Lynne Segal, Professor of Psychology and Gender Studies at Birkbeck College (*Guardian*, 26/2/2004)

The feminist author of *The Feminine Mystique* had barely been dead two minutes before others saw fit to get out their knives. A round-up of tributes from other feminists went from the ridiculous – 'When I heard about her death I picked up *The Feminine Mystique* and felt like throwing myself down on my knees and thanking her ghost for all she and her cohorts of passionate feminists did to save us from the prison of enforced femininity' (Natasha Walter) to the downright mean – 'Were it not for her politics, women like me wouldn't be able to appreciate how important radicalism is. She was such a wet, pathetic liberal that she made us realise what we really needed for the movement to succeed – and it wasn't her approach – backstabbing women and pandering to men' (Julie Bindel). Germaine Greer was determined to set the record straight now that Friedan had given up her right to reply by dying:

'She would become breathless with outrage if she didn't get the deference she thought she deserved . . . Betty was not one to realise that she was being lifted on an existing wave; she thought she was the wave, that she had actually created the Zeitgeist that was ready and hungry for her book . . . Betty's Zeitgeist was not mine . . . *The Female Eunuch* was conceived in reaction to the *Feminine Mystique*.'

Guardian, 7/2/2006

Ariel Levy is thirty-odd years old, a lifestyle journalist and contributing editor to *New York* magazine. Her book

*Female Chauvinist Pigs: Women and the Rise of Raunch
Culture* published in Britain only in paperback, is a modest
workman-like assemblage of cut-and-pasted lifestyle pieces
that have appeared in the magazine under various titles,
dating back as far as 1999. In England this unassuming
little book has been hailed as a new feminist bible,
launching a slew of articles about our culture's fascination
with porn stars, silicone breasts and lap dancing which all
raise the question, 'Is this what women's liberation was
supposed to be about?' In the US her book has been hailed
as 'The Fall of Feminism'. It can't very well be both; it is
far more likely to be neither.

Germaine Greer (*Sunday Times*, 2/7/2006)

The bitchiest thing that anyone has ever done to me
was when I was agony aunt on the *Sunday Mirror*
and Marje Proops was the saintly agony aunt on the
Daily Mirror. We were friends and she made out that
she was always on my side. Then suddenly I got
sacked and found out that she had taken my job.
The sense of betrayal by this ambitious woman was
immense and she was so two-faced about it. She
rang and said 'Oh, Virginia, I've been trying to get
hold of you all day,' (which wasn't true) 'I was forced
into it,' she said, 'I couldn't say no.' I didn't speak to
her for ages and then we arranged a conciliatory
lunch. On the very day of that lunch I read an
interview with her in a book by Naim Attallah in
which she said, 'Virginia was sacked because she

was so useless.' I shouldn't have gone at all but I did and sat there feeling so sick. But I can't have been that bad because after she died I was rehired.

Virginia Ironside

Mothers and Daughters

You will have a great deal of unreserved discourse
with Mrs K., I dare say, upon this subject, as well as
upon many other of our family matters. Abuse
everybody but me.

Jane Austen in a letter to her sister Cassandra,
7 January 1807

As with everything, the roots of bitching are formed within the
family. The dynamics of family life mean that individuals are
more aware of each other's weaknesses and can slander each
other with comments that would render them friendless outside the family. Yet the great strength of family is that whatever
you say, the blood link remains and *most* of the time relationships are sustained, though not always, and family feuds are the
most lethal. Sisters can be notoriously rivalrous, envying each
other's advantages and competing with each other for status
and success in the world and within the family, and that usually manifests itself with the veiled, tangential put-down which
typifies bitching. 'But I always thought you wanted to die,' my
mother-in-law said to her elder sister one lunch-time when she
expressed concern about eating eggs during the Salmonella
crisis.

Once again principles of evolutionary psychology, with people competing for scarce resources, holds sway, only this time it is children of both sexes competing for parental love, attention and approval which lies at the root of sibling rivalry. Child psychiatrist Judy Dunn has discovered that children as young as twelve months are sensitive to disputes and the relationship between parents and their siblings. 'Children are far more socially sophisticated than we ever imagined,' she says. 'That little fifteen-month-old is watching like a hawk what goes on between her mother and older sibling and the greater the difference in the maternal affection and attention, the more hostility and conflict between the siblings' (*Psychology Today*, Jan/Feb 1993). Try as they might, parents often have favourite children and the acute antennae of a small child pick this up. By the age of three, a child will have grasped how to manipulate the social politics of their family to their own advantage and rivalrous relationships with siblings soon develop. They learn how to push each other's buttons and in later life that competitive instinct for survival can resurface at seismic moments in family life – weddings, the birth of a child or when a parent gets ill or dies.

The root of all bitching between girls and women has to lie buried deep somewhere within that highly complex relationship between mothers and daughters. Our mothers exert a powerful force over the whole of our lives. We can always hear their voice, feel the touch of their skin and see their faces. We absorb their values and their mannerisms, and their words and phrases unwittingly pop out from our own mouths. There are more fights between mothers and daughters than there are in any other familial relationship, largely because of resentment, insecurity, envy and high expectations. 'Look what the cat brought in!' said a friend's mother when she brought round her new boyfriend. 'My mother is so evil she sent me a sympathy card on my wedding day,' says a woman on an Internet chatroom.

Often it isn't the words but the tone with which they are delivered. The simple question 'When am I going to see you?' is weighted with meaning and resentment. Appearance looms high on many a mother's hit list. She runs her eyes up and down her daughter's clothes and says absolutely nothing at all, or worse, when they do: 'I don't like you in short sweaters, you should wear long ones. And if you permed your hair I'm sure you'd have found a man by now,' as one elderly mother recently said to a friend, who is widowed and in her fifties.

Daughters can be hypersensitive to the nuances of what's not being said as well as what is being said because they know their mothers so intimately. They have watched them intensely during their childhood and often know their mothers better than they know themselves. The simple statement, 'I went over to see your cousin Clare today,' heaves with innuendo when you know from past experience that your mother has always got on with Clare better than she has with you. Or always admired her cooking, sense of style and the way her own children excel at every single one of the arts as well as Maths and Science. It doesn't matter how grown-up you are, one's mother always has the ability to reduce one to the raw emotion of feeling unloved, small or unappreciated and searching for that same sense of approval as one did as a child. If you have the sort of mother who will not give you what you need, you grow so used to the drip-drip of bitchy criticism laced with love, that you learn how to push the humiliation to one side rather than risk a fight by rising to it. Even if it is a good relationship, it can be intense and emotional and the bitching can go both ways. It's just what mothers do. It's just what girls do. There is a 'sense in which you can get away with it,' says Stephanie Lawler, author of *Mothering the Self*. 'The maternal persona is about love that doesn't have to be reciprocated. Of course they're not all caring, all loving but it is difficult for a mother not to inhabit that persona and for a daughter consequently to feel its okay to bitch more at their mothers.'

Tensions between mothers and daughters are inevitably exacerbated by the vast differences in expectation and achievement between generations of women. For some, the fact that their daughters don't want to get married or have children, or become high-achieving working mothers, or are lesbians is so contrary to everything they have experienced that they find it hard to approve. For others, their own ambitions were so compromised by the pressure to marry and have children that they feel a deep resentment of the choice and freedoms their daughters now have. Self-sacrificing mothers dominate their daughters through their martyrdom and make it hard to establish a more equal relationship as adults. Daughters feel guilty about not being able to or wanting to give as much back and resent the expectation that they should. It's also less easy to be genuinely outspoken, triumphant and happy about their achievements when they are afraid of arousing that latent just-below-the-surface envy in their mothers, that stiffening of posture followed by the barbed put-down that implies that one shouldn't boast or be proud. Once again, a strong sense of self plays a key part. When mothers feel content with their lives, they envy their daughters less and allow them to thrive as separate individuals who can give freely. When they feel vulnerable they tend to get a bit spiky.

It is in early adolescence, when daughters first start to try and differentiate themselves from their mothers, that the first rows and ructions emerge and become more intense and hostile than at any other time in their relationship. Girls want to assert themselves; mothers resent losing their affectionate little girl and try and reassert their authority and the arguments easily spiral out of control. 'The daughter wants to step out of the role her mother expects and be the bad girl who shocks,' says Terri Apter, 'and then when the mother bitches back it's usually because she is at her wits' end and has lost control.' Sally is an attractive blonde in her forties who used to be a model and an actress. Looking good matters to her. So that's exactly where her daughter hits. 'She says I'm old in front of people, particularly men, so I call her spotty, and then she'll slam the door and say I'm a bitch – but it's okay for her to say I'm old! If I tell her off about her clothes or her make-up not being suitable, she'll say I'm old and jealous of her. We were on a train once, and I was putting the case up on the rack. My trousers slipped a bit so you could see the top of my g-string, if you looked. So my daughter says at the top of her voice, so everyone heard and looked, "Why are you dressed like a teenager? I can see your thong." I had to really keep my mouth shut because otherwise I knew I'd say something so horrible that we'd have a massive fight.'

It is mothers with the strongest sense of self, contentment and individual achievement who feel least rejected by adolescent daughters and more able to recognise that there is still mutual need and love. Those that manage to limit their rivalry with adolescent daughters tend to have better relationships once their daughters grow up because there is less for either to resent or envy. A close loving relationship is earned rather than a natural by-product of giving birth. The looks and lives of mothers and daughters feel so entwined that daughters often feel they have to attack their mothers to push them far enough away so that they can breath and live their own lives. That may feel like rejection, but only if you depend too much on the relationship for emotional support which you should be getting from elsewhere. As young women, daughters spend a great deal of time thinking about all of the ways they are different to their mothers. But as they grow older and become mothers them-selves, they are reminded, daily, of their similarities – and that can be horrifying.

My own mother is a talented writer and therefore can be wicked with words. Over the years we've had many a spat, par-ticularly when I was a teenager and living under the same roof. Now that I'm older, and more confident about my own strengths as distinct from hers, I've got better at withdrawing when I sense a bitchathon looming, although that can still be hard even in middle age. One humorous recent anecdote where my mother unwittingly triumphed will suffice. It was Mothering Sunday and as I walked the dog in the morning I rang my mother to wish her a happy Mother's Day. At lunchtime I was doing a session at Jewish Book Week with Allison Pearson and Michele Hanson on Jewish mothers. When I revealed this my mother said, 'I looked at the programme for Jewish Book Week and there seemed to me to be a dearth of really good writers there this year.' Ouch. I didn't hit back with anything, just brought the conversation swiftly to an end, smarting slightly at the insult, and laughed at her audacity. The event went well until it came to signing our books. Allison and Michele sat down behind a large pile of copies. Mine were nowhere to be seen. I sat down, furious, at an empty table while the bookshop tried anxiously to find them. Then one sweet lady took pity on me. She approached the table hesitantly with a copy of one of my mother's books, which clearly were in plentiful supply. 'I wondered if you'd like to sign this for me,' she said.

'Ah . . .' I said, 'I didn't write that book, my mother did.'

'I know,' replied the woman. 'But could you sign it all the same, for your mother?'

~

Veda (Ann Blyth) is the seventeen-year-old only daughter of Mildred Pierce (Joan Crawford). Mildred has worked hard as a single mother to give her daughter everything . . . but she's spoilt and she wants more. She borrows money from her mother's employees, threatening them with dismissal if they turn her down, and then marries a young millionaire to get an annulment settlement out of his mother. She waves the cheque in her mother's face . . .

VEDA: With this money I can get away from *you* – from you
        and your chickens and your pies and your kitchens and
        everything that smells of grease. I can get away from
        this shack with its cheap furniture and this town and its
        dollar-days and its women that wear uniforms and its
        men that wear overalls.

MILDRED: Veda, I think I'm really seeing you for the first time in my life and you're cheap and horrible . . .

VEDA: (*venomously hateful*) You think that just because you made a little money you can get a new hair-do and some expensive clothes and turn yourself into a lady, but you can't because you'll never be anything but a common frump whose father lived over a grocery store and whose mother took in washing. With this money I can get away from every rotten stinking thing that makes me think of this place or you!

Mildred Pierce, 1945

Limiting the Damage

My daughter expected me to buy her a T-shirt with the words 'If you think I'm a bitch, wait until you meet my mother.' I didn't

'Good' mothers sacrifice themselves at the altar of their child. 'Good' mothers are expected to give up their lives and their pleasures and devote themselves to nurturing their young. And we do. We love and nourish them with every cell of our being because we want to, because there's little choice but to when the needs of small children are so immediate and there is very little time or energy left for ourselves.

The trouble with the 'Good Mother' paradigm is that it is unachievable, so there are times, often daily, when we feel as if we have failed and are therefore 'bad' mothers – when we shout or lose our temper, when we feel profound loathing, even hate. When we cannot respond positively with a smile to every single verbal statement, when we fail to make a good enough costume for the nativity play, when we haven't sent them to extra-curricular classes or helped them with their home-work . . . The list is endless, add one of your own. Even when we are astute enough to recognise the fact that we cannot ever be perfect mothers, we still aim for those illusive heights and punish ourselves when we inevitably fail. We strive silently to do better by our own beloved children than the next woman. The competitive spirit nurtured from early adolescence over appearance, attention and men, zooms into fifth gear when it comes to our children. That pushiness is then justified as a primary instinctive urge to protect them from predators by equipping them with essential skills for survival in an increasingly competitive world.

And to some extent that instinct is right, largely because of the way the job description of motherhood has expanded so radically. It is no longer enough just to keep our young alive, fed and clothed until they reach adulthood. We now know so much more about what children need to thrive, even in the womb, and mothers take it upon themselves to nurture every aspect of their child's emotional, psychological and educational welfare. Yet when mothers openly push their children, they lay themselves open to criticism, and when mothers fail to provide what many of us now consider to be the essentials, they also get put down. The hierarchy of perfect mother down to bad mother exists in every mother's head, just as the pecking order of most attractive Queen Bee to plain saddo does amongst teenage girls.

Mothers and daughters have the most intense, symbiotic relationship. When it's good, it can be warm and emotionally nourishing; when it's bad, mothers and daughters can make each other's lives miserable with the most brutal bitchfights imaginable. Both the good and the bad stem from this inexorable symbiosis. One cannot deny that link unless you choose to cut off the relationship completely. But you can limit the damage caused by the bitchfights if you choose to reinterpret what's being said and why.

Mothers give their daughters the greatest gift imaginable when they have enough of a sense of self and contentment to allow their daughters to flourish as individuals. When mothers feel vulnerable or insecure they are more likely to feel envious or resent what their daughters have, and they are much more likely to foster sibling rivalry by attempting to divide and rule. So if the words that fly between you feel hurtful and destructive, take a long hard look at yourself and what you feel is lacking in your life rather than at what your daughter is or isn't doing/saying. When daughters are adolescent, the onus is on mothers to remain the parent at all times and limit damaging conflict. All families experience more rows once their children become teenagers; they're hormonal, emotionally volatile, coping with a great deal of physical, emotional and psychological change and they get stressed easily. It's healthy and normal to row occasionally over everything from tidying bedrooms to exam revision. Rows help teenagers to confirm their views and differentiate themselves and they enable new boundaries and compromises for both parent and child.

But often, when mothers feel unsure of themselves or unhappy with their lot, rows with their teenage daughters become unhealthy, tinged with ridicule, humiliation and distortion. 'Conflict gets nasty when the mother's agenda or needs are perceived as being the only ones that count and when the daughter isn't given enough space. Without negotiation or compromise teenage daughters easily feel helpless, humiliated and childlike, which is not what an adolescent girl wants to feel when she is trying to grow up,' says adolescent psychotherapist Jeannie Milligan. 'Bad conflict comes when there is bitterness, when hurting the other person is more important than compromise,' says Dorothy Rowe. When arguments get this personal, they can quickly spiral out of control and turn into bitchathon slanging matches where nobody wins and everybody feels upset and unloved.

If your daughter says things like 'You never listen to me,' or 'You don't love me,' when you're arguing, then you're fast approaching meltdown and it's time to take control if you value your relationship with her. Think about what you're about to say so that anything that could be interpreted as critical gets stifled. Never criticise her appearance – she always looks 'lovely' even when she is covered in spots. Teenagers are so sensitive and if your relationship is plummeting to these depths, almost anything you say is bound to be interpreted in the wrong way. She needs to know that she always looks lovely, at least to you. When she shouts at you, don't shout back, she'll hear your anger not the words. Listen to what she has to say – let her rant and really listen so that you can respond appropriately and reassure her. This is not about you but about her, a troubled teen who still needs your love and maternal care. Pick your fights carefully – what a teenager wears, her friends, the state of her room, and how long she spends on the telephone are private matters and far less important than issues of education or health and safety which fall within the parameters of your responsibility as a parent. And be alert to white flags during rows, changing the subject or the slightest concession on her part must be pounced on as the end of the matter. Don't go on and make things worse.

If mothers handle the teen years sensitively, they stand a much better chance of forging a closer relationship with their daughters as adults. And once daughters have grown up, the onus is on them as much as on mothers to limit the bitching, by understanding where it's coming from and looking to their own sensitivities and insecurities. When you feel as if your mother is constantly criticising your appearance, your values, your skills as a parent, try and rethink that criticism as evidence of caring. She doesn't necessarily mean to be nasty, she just wants you to look/be your best. And when your mother says something which hurts your feelings, ask her what she actually means by that rather than simply snapping back with an even more hurtful retort. Open the way for a different type of dialogue, rather than sticking to the historical tram-lines of your relationship. And if she says something which you know is meant to be hurtful, tell her so, be honest, say 'It really hurts me when you talk like that about . . .', rather than bitching back. By reacting differently, you lessen the sting. By changing the way you speak to your mother, you change the way she speaks to you. Talking about how you talk can be a powerful way of stepping out of the situation and viewing it from the outside. 'It helps if both mothers and daughters step back and see the other person as if they were not related to them,' says Dr Stephanie Lawler, author of *Mothering the Self*. 'You might still think, "I hate her guts" but so much is bound up in that relationship that it helps to take the intensity and the heat off.'

Often the real problem is just that mothers and daughters spend much too much time talking to each other about the deeply personal minutiae of daily life rather than doing things together so that they have something else to talk about. By doing you become – one of the most valuable lessons we can pass on to our own daughters. When girls are encouraged to pursue their own interests, hobbies, desires and ambitions, they develop a firmer sense of self, of who they are and what they like. As they grow up and with this firmer sense of self, they are less likely to feel the need to put other women down. We need to encourage our daughters to be loud, honest and outspoken, able to contribute to debate without fearing that their whole personality will be trashed when someone disagrees with them. They need to be kind and considerate of others but not to the point of self-denial. We all need to be able to look after ourselves confidently before we can help others. And we need to ease off the pressure to be feminine – to look good, be thin, have nice hair, because they get more than enough of that from the outside world and need to feel that their mothers love and accept them however they are. If they try too hard to be the 'Perfect', 'Good' girl they are destined for disappointment, because to be 'Perfect' means you can never get cross or be the 'bad' girl without feeling guilty or as if you have failed. Our daughters are entitled to pursue their dreams with confidence and all of the skills that we can provide them with as mothers. That means highlighting and destroying the age-old stereotypes, which confine as well as define us.

How Parents Can Help

As adults we know that it is quality of friendship that matters, not how many friends you have. The sooner you learn that lesson, the less time you waste at parties you don't want to be at and supporting 'friends' who rarely support you. Young people spend the best part of their teenage years learning how to manage and maintain mature relationships with their friends. They test each other out, exploring their emotional resilience, their ability to tolerate cruelty as well as be cruel and the philosophical significance of loyalty and betrayal. Often they make terrible mistakes, which they learn from. Bitching is part of that process. But there is a great deal that parents can do to help. If you think your child is being ostracised or hurt by friends at school but she doesn't want to talk about it, turn over this book and discover in *The Big Fat Bitch Book For Girls* just how cruel girlworld can be. Then consider some or all of the following . . .

It's not a question of having to choose between total withdrawal, allowing a child to 'toughen up' and complete intervention on her behalf. It's an alchemy, a mixture of both, which can change from day to day depending on what is happening and how upset a girl is. 'You don't toughen up just by ignoring something,' says Jennifer, a mother of three daughters, one of whom was isolated by friends for the best part of a year when they lived in France. 'Being sensitive to things is a quality. Pain lets us know when things aren't right and if you stop hurting you don't react anymore, and then you've really got a problem. But to think that the world is falling apart because you're hurting isn't right either. The world has to be bigger than your problems.' And that's where parents can help. Putting the issue into perspective, offering buckets of sympathy and understanding and providing constructive solutions.

We can't fight their battles for them, children need to work things out for themselves – but they do need plenty of guidance and advice. Be aware that girls tend to turn to their parents for help with their friendships more readily than boys. They may not want resolution so much as validation from you for their actions. They may also not be telling you the whole story. It's much harder for parents to accept that their daughters could be being cruel or bitchy to others because girls get so good at masking out the 'bad' bits. But adults also bring their own delusions to the table – by persisting in seeing their daughters as angels and 'good' girls because they have absorbed that message for women so effectively themselves. Acknowledging that girls could be contributing to their own difficulties by being the bitch, means accepting that they may have more difficulties than they can deal with, and that's often hard for parents.

If your daughter says she hasn't got any friends or that her friends are not being nice to her, don't belittle her comments with 'You've got loads of friends' or 'Just ignore them'. Take it seriously and listen. 'Let them offload as you would with a flatmate,' says Dr Begum Maitra, Consultant Child and Adolescent Psychiatrist. The most important thing you can offer is sanctuary at home. Often that is all they need. Let them know that you are willing to help and that nothing they will tell you will shock you (and then practice composure in case it does!).

Offer strategies and constructive suggestions such as those in the etiquette section of *The Big Fat Bitch Book for Girls*. Help them to practise through role-playing what they might say back or how to agree with the bully in order to deflate their attacks. A girl should always confront another about what she has been saying or doing in a one-to-one situation, where the other girl has no fear of losing face by apologising in front of other friends. Help her by talking through or writing down what she didn't like and what happened and what she would like to happen now, so that she can approach the other girl with greater confidence. Teach her about body language – help her to stand tall and ooze confidence even if that's fake. Buy some of the clothes they need to compete adequately so that they don't stand out as too different. Don't give them old-fashioned haircuts. Don't let them get overweight or unhealthy and become a target. Image is everything for a teenage girl, even though it shouldn't be.

Don't do anything proactive like going into school or ringing other girls' parents unless you have got your child's permission to do so. This will only make the situation worse. She will feel doubly betrayed rather than supported and will gain an additional reputation as someone who cannot sort out her own fights. Instead get the facts straight. Write things down. Give your daughter a notebook so that she can write down who says what, when, how she feels, what she'd like to say/do back. Firstly, that helps you both to pinpoint exactly what is going on. And if the problem exacerbates you have a record, which you can take in to show the school. If the problem doesn't go away, go in and explain calmly to your daughter's form teacher how 'relational aggression' can be more painful and prolonged than other more well-known forms of bullying. Ask what policy the school has to deal with this and suggest a generalised approach such as group discussions in PSHE. Bullying is often effectively dealt with by bringing in outside specialist drama groups, encouraging children to role-play. Women stand by and just take it too often in life. Often the main reason why we say 'It's up to the kids to sort it out,' is because we're scared of the confrontation too. The more we as parents draw schools' attention to the hidden and hurtful behaviour of girls, the more likely they are to take this very destructive form of bullying seriously. You're not just helping your own daughter, you're doing all girls a favour.

Encourage activities where your child is valued more for the contribution they make rather than what they are wearing or watching. Active participation in something gives teenagers welcome relief from the awful stress of feeling as if they are on show all the time and being judged for passive attributes. It also teaches them that there is more to life than being popular. Build up as many out of school activities as you can where children can meet other groups of friends and form relationships with other adults they may want to confide in. Teenagers need many more adults in their lives as role models and friends than they usually get.

We are more aware as parents of the importance of building their self-esteem, but if that self-esteem is not rooted in genuine self-awareness as to where their true strengths and abilities lie, that sense of self is fragile and easily threatened by reality. Overemphasising traditional 'feminine' attributes such as looks and clothes turns our daughters into dolls. It places them on precarious pedestals from which they are bound to fall when they compare themselves to the extreme ideals of models such as Kate Moss and find themselves wanting. It makes girls more vulnerable than they need to be, hypersensitive to criticism, which in turns makes them reluctant to seek out or hear wider views, which may contradict those false truths or tell them something they don't want to hear.

The importance of resilience is not recognised enough. We love our children so much that we want to protect them from disappointments and failures. But they need to experience controlled knocks in early childhood in order to be able to deal with the bigger knocks they will inevitably face as adolescents. 'It starts with resilience in the mother, not feeling the need to rush to her baby whenever it cries or to a small child whenever they fall over,' says child psychotherapist Jeannie Milligan. 'When you hold back just a little the child recognises the feelings from before and begins to understand that you can feel bad, but that it can get better. I know of one girl who was completely idolised by her mother. She was the Queen Bee at school. Then when two new girls came in the second year and starting bitching about her, this girl's entire structure crumbled. Why was this so lacerating? Because she had never been allowed to build resilience. Spoiling your child means you are spoiling their chances of being able to withstand negative situations and mean nastiness in the middle of the spectrum, or catastrophes at the end.'

Encouraging children to have a go at anything and experiencing the emotions that go with failure when it all goes wrong helps to build resilience. It teaches children that it's OK to fail and not feel humiliated by failure, that you don't have to be perfect, that things go wrong, in which case you pick yourself up again *without* your parents stepping in to sort things out for you the whole time.

Spoiling children doesn't just mean giving them everything they want. It also means not giving in to the things that they don't want to do, allowing them not to eat vegetables because they say they don't like them or not to do something that might be important for others (like visiting Granny, or writing thank-you notes) just because they would rather do something else. Through an element of denial and delayed gratification, children learn greater patience and tolerance. They also learn that their needs and wants cannot always be paramount. Manners are crucial if children are to learn how to respect others as distinct and different individuals which is now more crucial than ever given the ethnic mix of our schools. Having discussions at home where you encourage children to take or think about another person's point of view will encourage empathy. With more respect for differences in people, children are less likely to think that they can get their own way by bitching about others or bullying.

Competition in any form with clear rules and team spirit allows children to experience winning and losing and allows girls to be competitive and express their aggression in healthy ways. Competition is an essential component to one of the most essential and difficult tasks of adolescence – forming that crucial sense of individual self. It is only by comparing themselves to others of the same age that children develop a sense of who they are, their strengths and weaknesses and who they would like to be. Activities such as martial arts, self-defence and kick-boxing give girls an extra confidence and knowledge about what their bodies can do and how strong they actually are. They also encourage girls to take up more of the physical space around them, in the same way that boys do. Girls tend to shrink back unconsciously, nurture residual resentment at having to do so and then lash out verbally. Maybe teenage girls should be encouraged to express negative emotions in more constructive ways from an early age – through sport, open competition with clearly defined rules, drama activities and by punching cushions.

Don't push your daughter towards the children you think they should play with because of your own aspirations for them. We all want our kids to feel accepted but don't assume that by being popular all their problems will be solved. They may seem like the 'nice', popular girls from good homes to you, but your daughter may not feel comfortable with them. Let her choose her own friends.

Talk about what friendship means and how important it is to work at friendships that matter to you – that means consideration, apologies and most importantly forgiveness when they make mistakes, for often friendships grow stronger and closer after a fall-out.

Discuss how there is such pressure on girls to be 'perfect' – pretty, nice, kind, selfless, not too clever and never angry – and how hard it can be sometimes to maintain that fiction. Encourage girls to widen the definition of what it means to be female so that it encompasses human individuality, not ideals of femininity. And do you as a parent add to that pressure by encouraging her to dress in more feminine ways or not to talk back? Do you tolerate abusive behaviour at home from a husband or parent and communicate the message to your daughter that it's OK to put up with it? 'Good' girls take everything on the chin. They turn into women who are more likely to get paid less than men because they're either too scared to ask for a rise or assume their boss is being fair. They turn into working mothers who end up doing the bulk of the housework and childcare because that's what they feel 'good' mothers should do. If you have the confidence to speak out against injustice, to talk back, to be assertive, you are much less likely to ever be the victim. And it is only by encouraging girls to be open and honest with each other about how they really feel that they will begin to learn the important lesson that we should be able to confront our friends when they piss us off without fearing that you will lose that relationship completely. In homes where issues such as sexism and racism are discussed, girls are more likely to question, speak out and are less scared by rifts in relationships. Talk about how little truth there is in the gossip and bitching we hear and see around us – in papers, magazines, television and school.

Don't overreact emotionally if your daughter is a target. Children feel safer if they sense that their parents know what to do. If they see you incredibly upset or angry about this, they feel responsible for you and for your welfare when it needs to be the other way around. If you get over-emotional about it question why. If you were bullied, excluded or bitched about as a child then similar hostilities experienced by your own daughter will be doubly painful. Talk about what happened to you, how you coped, how you are more resilient as a result. And if dredging up these memories is too traumatic seek help by ringing an organisation such as Parentline (0808 800 2222).

It can be harder to accept that your daughter is actually the 'bitch' rather than the victim. It may be a relief to know that she isn't being overly upset by others but there are equally damaging repercussions to being the bitch. I was particularly struck by a passage in Daniel Goleman's book on social intelligence where he talks about the 'Dark Triad' of narcissists, Machiavellians and psychopaths. 'All three share to varying degrees an unappealing, though sometimes well-concealed core: social malevolence and duplicity, self-centredness and aggression, and emotional coldness. We could do well to familiarise ourselves with the hallmarks of this threesome, if only to better recognise them. Modern society, with its me-first motives glorified, celebrity demi-gods of greed unleashed and vanity idealised, may be inadvertently inviting these types to flourish. Most people who fall into the Dark Triad do not qualify for a psychiatric diagnosis, though at their extremes they shade into mental illness or become outlaws – particularly the psychopath. But the far more common 'subclinical' variety live among us, populating offices, schools, bars and the routine by-ways of daily life.'

If cruelty is not being challenged effectively at school and society perpetuates selfish greed and ill-mannered bitchy behaviour, the onus is on us as parents to challenge it at home. The more we foster empathy and concern for others in our children, the less anti-social they are likely to be as adults. They are also likely to be happier, with more nourishing and supportive relationships with friends and lovers. If your daughter exhibits all the signs of being popular then she could be targeting other more vulnerable girls. Ask her if there is any bitching at school. If she says there isn't, it's probably because she doesn't find herself at the receiving end and in all likelihood downplays her own nastiness, understandably. Talk generally about how you respond to people that irritate you, what insults such as 'slut' or 'whore' really mean and how important it is to check what you say, why bitching hurts and how scared we are of honest confrontation. Don't model bad behaviour by gossiping or bitching about others in front of her. And if you hear from other parents that your daughter is very popular, the Queen Bee, try not to smirk. It's not actually a compliment. When girls need to surround themselves with the false construct of popularity they are usually trying to protect an inner weaker core. You would do better by her as a parent if you took a long hard look at the influences on your daughter's life and considered ways in which you could bolster true inner strength and resilience.

Girls are wonderful. They're not just capable of great kindnesses and understanding, they're clever, dynamic, funny, athletic individuals with amazing psychological resilience. They care about each other and they depend upon each other for emotional support and their social life. They are also so much better at resolving conflicts than boys that they can work things out, provided they understand *why* they bitch, and when there are enough adults around to guide them. 'Teenage girls have such a terrible reputation for bitching and it would be so great if you could just get rid of that and see how everything else they do is so good. I love my school and the girls in it are so kind and supportive to each other, they're really lovely people.' Lily, fifteen.

By openly discussing the stereotypes of 'good' and 'bad' girl, misogyny and sexism, how girls repress emotions such as anger and competition and the ways in which women need and can support each other in the wider world, we give them the confidence to be the fabulous individuals they are, comfortable in their own skins and able to focus more on their strengths than their weaknesses. It starts in the playground. When parents and teachers confront these stereotypes and give girls an understanding of why they bitch, we give them a model for a different way of working – together rather than as rivals.

Top Bitch Viewing

Joan Crawford: Douglas Fairbanks introduced me to the great plays, and Franchoit taught me what they *mean*. He taught me words like 'metaphor' and 'transference'.

Jean Harlow: And she taught him words like 'jump' and 'fuck'.

From *Bette and Joan – The Divine Feud*
by Shaun Considine

~

When I'm good I'm very, very good, but when I'm bad, I'm better.

Mae West

Twentieth-century cinema would be pretty dull without its bad girls, the schemers, double crossers and temptresses, the femmes fatales and bitches of the silver screen. Bette Davis, Joan Crawford, Barbara Stanwyck, Margaret Lockwood, Katharine Hepburn, Mae West and Greta Garbo are just some of the powerful women with razor-sharp scripts and wits who dominated the movies from the first talkies of the thirties to the fifties in particular. These 'bad' girls had all of the best parts and lines. Their characters drove the plot. They were ballsy women who stood up for themselves on screen and off. Here then is a roll-call of the top screen bitches and some of their greatest lines:

GRETA GARBO

Greta Garbo was steely cold, independent and determined. As the Russian agent in *Ninotchka* she is not impressed with the Eiffel Tower – 'Vat a vaste of electricity', she says. And when Lewis Stone expresses concern that she might die an old maid in *Queen Cristina* (1933) she replies haughtily, 'I have no intention to. I shall die a bachelor.'

NINOTCHKA: We don't have men like you in my country.
LEON: Thank you.
NINOTCHKA: That is why I believe in the future of my
    country.

BETTE DAVIS

Bette Davis played so many evil women, delivering her barbed lines in those harsh, clipped New England tones that she should rightfully be crowned as queen of the bitches. One critic even went so far as to say that if she had lived two or three hundred years ago, 'Bette Davis would probably have been burned as a witch.' Her first classic quote comes from *The Cabin in the Cotton* (1932) in which she says to Richard Barthelmess 'I'd love to kiss ya, but I jest washed ma hay-ur.' In *The Little Foxes* (1941) she plays the scheming, self centred Regina Giddens. In *Whatever Happened to Baby Jane*, the only film Davis was ever to star in with her arch rival Joan Crawford, it was Davis who suggested they substitute the dead parakeet she was supposed to serve to her invalid sister (Crawford) for a dead rat without telling her. The look of shock on Joan Crawford's face when she lifts the silver lid is genuine. But it is in *All About Eve* where she plays veteran movie bitch Margo Channing that she comes out with some of her best lines. Eve (Anne Baxter) is an ambitious young actress (and bitch) who worms her way into Channing's life with the aim of surpassing her. Channing has become a hardened bitch because of personal sacrifices she has had to make to succeed and because she fears being usurped at forty in a profession where youth and beauty matter most for a woman. 'Funny business, a woman's career, the things you drop on the way up the ladder so you can move faster. You forget you'll need them again when you get back to being a woman. It's one career all females have in common – being a woman. Sooner or later we've got to work at it no matter how many other careers we've had or wanted. And in the last analysis nothing is any good unless you can look up just before dinner or turn around in bed and there he is. Without that you're not a woman. You're something with a French provincial office or a book full of clippings but you're not a woman. Slow curtain, the end.'

'Shucks, and I sent my autograph book to the cleaner' (On being told that a Hollywood movie star has just arrived at her party)

Lovely speech, Eve. But I wouldn't worry so much about your heart. You can always put that award where your heart should be. (When Eve makes it and is awarded the 'Sarah Siddons Award')

JOAN CRAWFORD

Joan Crawford had a terrifying stare beneath those heavy eyebrows. As Bette Davis loved to point out regularly, she was born on the wrong side of the tracks, started performing as a showgirl and fought her way up to the top. The Women (1939) starred every top-tier female star at MGM except for Greta Garbo and Myrna Loy. There are some amusing bitchy lines from all of them but it was Crawford who excelled as the catty shop-girl Crystal Allen who is having an affair with Mary's husband Stephen. When Mary (Norma Shearer) confronts her and says that Stephen could never love a girl like her, Crystal replies, 'Well, if he can't, he's an awfully good actor . . . You noble wives and mothers bore the brains out of me. I'll bet you bore your husbands too.' When Mary suggests that the gold lamé Crystal is trying on is unsuitable for entertaining her husband, Crystal replies, 'When anything I wear doesn't please Stephen, I take it off.' Norma Shearer made Crawford change her costume sixteen times during the shooting of one scene. According to Crawford, 'Every one was prettier than hers.' Crawford did however thank her co-star for assisting on the set. 'I love to play bitches and Norma helped me in this part.'

Memorable lines from *The Women*

Sylvia Fowler (Rosalind Russell): You simply must see my hairdresser, I *detest* whoever does yours.

~

Edith Potter (Phyllis Povar) to Nancy Blake (Florence Nash): When do you go to Africa to shoot, dear?

Blake: As soon as my book is out.

Sylvia Fowler: I don't blame you. I'd rather face a tiger any day than the sort of things the critics said about your last book.

~

Edith Potter: What are you going to write next, Nancy? Animal stories?

Nancy (looking at Sylvia Fowler): Oh, I wouldn't have to go to Africa to do that.

~

Joan Crawford to Marilyn Monroe: You are very pretty, my dear, but you don't know shit about clothes.

BARBARA STANWYCK

Barbara Stanwyck came from a tough background. Her mother was the victim of a drunken manslaughter and Ruby (her real name) left school at thirteen and became a chorus girl at the age of fifteen. In all of her films, she's the toughy with the twisted smile who takes no shit from anybody. In *Baby Face* (1933) she climbs over man after man to get from the bottom of the company to the top, but it was her portrayal of sexy, pushy murderess Phyllis Dietrichson in *Double Indemnity* (1944) where her bitching qualities are best remembered. She is more than a match for Fred MacMurray, insurance salesman, persuading him to murder her husband.

PHYLLIS: Mr Neff, why don't you drop by tomorrow evening about 8:30. He'll be in then.

WALTER NEFF [MacMurray]: Who?

PHYLLIS: My husband. You were anxious to talk to him, weren't you?

WALTER NEFF: Yeah, I was, but I'm sort of getting over the idea if you know what I mean.

PHYLLIS: There's a speed limit in this state, Mr Neff. Forty-five miles an hour

WALTER NEFF: How fast was I going, officer?

PHYLLIS: I'd say around ninety.

WALTER NEFF: Suppose you get down off your motorcycle and give me a ticket.

PHYLLIS: Suppose I let you off with a warning this time.

WALTER NEFF: Suppose it doesn't take.

PHYLLIS: Suppose I have to whack you over the knuckles.

WALTER NEFF: Suppose I bust out crying and put my head on your shoulder.

PHYLLIS: Suppose you try putting it on my husband's shoulder.

WALTER NEFF: That tears it (*he takes his hat and briefcase after his advances are coldly rebuffed*) 8.30 tomorrow evening then.

PHYLLIS: That's what I suggested.

WALTER NEFF: You'll be here too?

PHYLLIS: I guess so, I usually am.

WALTER NEFF: Same chair? Same perfume? Same anklet?

PHYLLIS: I wonder if I know what you mean.

WALTER NEFF: (*at the entrance*) I wonder if you wonder.

Double Indemnity, **1944**

LANA TURNER

Lana Turner and Rita Hayworth were exotic temptresses. They oozed man-trapping sex appeal but were strong self-interested women underneath. Lana Turner's father was murdered when she was ten. She used her stunning looks to further her career, got nicknamed 'The Sweater Girl' after a long walk in a tight sweater in *They Won't Forget* (1937) and soon developed her own trademark – taking one puff on a cigarette before stubbing it out. But it was in *The Postman Always Rings Twice* (1946), the remake of *Double Indemnity*, that she produced her classic bitch part, persuading her handsome drifter lover to murder her older husband.

FRANK CHAMBERS: I can sell anything to anyone.

CORA SMITH: [Turner] That's what you think.

The Postman Always Rings Twice, **1946**

MARGARET LOCKWOOD

Margaret Lockwood was the big 'bad' girl of the British screen. She was a major box office force from 1938–1950. Her most famous role was as Lady Barbara in *The Wicked Lady* (1945), with the beauty spot on her left cheek that was to become her trademark. Her marriage is so dull she takes to highway robbery instead. She has an affair with fellow highwayman Jerry Jackson (played by James Mason) but robbery soon turns to murder. The critics hated this melodrama but audiences queued round the block to see it and it was the most successful British film of the year. She went on to play more 'bad' girls in *Bedelia* (1946) and *Jassy* (1947).

MAE WEST

Mae West and Jean Harlow were vampy bitches with wit. Mae West wrote much of her own material, went to prison after her play *Sex* was raided by police in 1927 and refused to bow to her critics by toning down her sexual ruderies. Her masterful innuendos such as 'Come up and see me sometime' and 'Is that a gun in your pocket or are you just pleased to see me?' are legendary. In her first Hollywood film *Night After Night* the hat-check girl says 'Goodness, what beautiful diamonds.' 'Goodness had nothing to do with it, dearie,' West quips back. In a list of fifteen 'Things I'll Never Do' by Mae West, which include 'cook, bake, sew, wear white cottons or join a nudist colony', number seven is interesting. 'Play mother parts, sad parts, dumb parts or a virtuous wife, betrayed or otherwise. I pity weak women, good or bad, but I can't like them. A woman should be strong either in her goodness or her badness.'

'May we ask what types of men you prefer?'

'Just two, domestic and foreign.'

'Where are you stopping during your visit here?'

'Stoppin' at nothin'.'

She Done Him Wrong – where West is surrounded
by fawning men asking questions outside a
gambling saloon

~

Mae West on Jayne Mansfield: I don't know anything about her except the common gossip I heard. When it comes to men I heard she never turns anything down except the bedcovers.

ELIZABETH TAYLOR

Elizabeth Taylor was a child star during the reign of 'bitch' stars Davis, Crawford and Stanwyck during the 1940s, so she had plenty of good role models. She parodies Bette Davis at the start of her academy award-winning performance as drunken, blowsy Martha in the screen version of Edward Albee's *Who's Afraid of Virginia Woolf?* (1966) when she looks dismissively around her living room and says 'What a dump!' – the line used by Davis in *Beyond the Forest* (1949), 'I'm loud and I'm vulgar and I wear the pants in the house because somebody's got to, but I'm no monster' she spits at her husband George (played by Richard Burton) during their all-night row, where they humiliate each other publicly in front of another couple played by George Segal and Sandy Dennis. And yet they love each other. Near the end of the film, as dawn breaks, Martha confesses, 'There's only been one man in my whole life who's made me happy . . . George.' Martha is a bitch because she's miserable and disappointed. They have an invented sixteen-year-old son because they couldn't have children and George has failed to take over her father's role as president of the university.

MARTHA: So anyway, I married the S.O.B and I had it all planned out . . . he was the groom . . . he was going to be groomed. He'd take over some day . . . first, he'd take over the History department, and then, when Daddy retired, he'd take over the college . . . you know? That's the way it was supposed to be. (*To George, who is at the portable bar with his back to her*) You getting angry, baby? Hunh? (*Now back*) That's the way it was *supposed* to be. Very simple. And Daddy seemed to think it was a pretty good idea too. For a while. Until he watched for a couple of years! (*To George again*) You getting angrier? (*Now back*) Until he watched for a couple of years and started thinking maybe it wasn't such a good idea after all . . . that maybe Georgie boy didn't have the *stuff* . . . that he didn't have it in him!

GEORGE: (*still with his back to them all*) Stop it, Martha.

MARTHA: (*viciously triumphant*) The hell I will! You see George didn't have much . . . push . . . he wasn't particularly aggressive. In fact he was sort of a . . . (*spits the word at George's back*) . . . *a flop!* A great . . . big . . . fat . . . *flop!*

KATHLEEN TURNER

Kathleen Turner and Sharon Stone stand out as rare jewels of contemporary 'bitch' cinema. Turner's debut was in *Body Heat* (1981), a loose remake of the *Double Indemnity* story, only this time it's Turner's character Matty who is the double-crosser, who tries to kill both men to keep all the money. 'You aren't too bright, I like that in a man,' she says to Ned, played by William Hurt. She also mastered comic 'bitch-mode' in *The Man with Two Brains* (1983) and *The War of the Roses* (1989). She made a dramatic comeback to the London stage in 2006, playing Martha in *Who's Afraid of Virginia Woolf?*

MATTY: My temperature runs a couple of degrees high, around a hundred. I don't mind. It's the engine or something.

NED: Maybe you need a tune-up.

MATTY: Don't tell me. You have just the right tool.

Body Heat, 1981

JOAN COLLINS

Joan Collins has consistently done the bad girl proud. She was the scheming second wife of Pharaoh Jack Hawkins in *Land of the Pharaohs* (1955). She was cast in Joan Crawford's shoes, as the hard-nosed Crystal in *The Opposite Sex*, the 1956 remake of *The Women*. She also starred in two films based on the novels by her sister Jackie Collins – *The Stud* (1978) and *The Bitch* (1979). But it was as Alexis Morrell Carrington Colby Dexter Rowan – überbitch in the 1980s television soap *Dynasty* where she became a loveable international star of the bitches with some memorable lines: 'If I am [a bitch], take a lesson from me, you may need it in life' (to Kirby Colby) and 'You've won this round . . . but the night is still young' (Alexis to Krystle after a catfight in the fountain). 'I don't regret *The Stud*,' she said, 'because it was a renaissance for me. I did regret *The Bitch*; I hated the script and quality-wise it was a disaster. It also saddled me with that goddamn label . . .'

Joan Collins reviewing the 2001 Oscars in the *Spectator*.

The Singer Bjork was persuaded to dress as a dying swan, complete with lolling head and beak, in a creation that wouldn't have looked out of place perched on a Skegness landlady's spare loo roll. Juliette Binoche was being strangled by a surfeit of faux-pearl necklaces, cascading down her chest to her thighs and hideous Toulouse-Lautrec laced-up boots. But the full horror was . . . Pamela Anderson. Revealing all the taste and refinement of a hooker on holiday, she chose to buck the system in denim hot pants and a teeny-weeny white shirt which struggled bravely to contain her.

Top Bitch Reading

THE WICKED STEPMOTHER

There are more than 900 folk tales featuring a wicked step-mother. She is always portrayed as evil personified, the big bad witch, for all children fear the dangers that would come from losing their real mother. The child is innocent, good and always triumphs at the end of the story. The wicked stepmother is self-centred and intent upon furthering the interests of her own children, and often casts out or humiliates the stepchild as in Cinderella. They can be jealous of the child's beauty, youth and attention from the father, as in 'Snow White'. They often display the same personality traits as witches, as in Hansel and Gretel (the children kill the witch and then when they get back home the stepmother is dead as well). Female stereotypes of 'good' and 'bad' girl begin with the wicked stepmother. All fairy tales sim-plify complex emotions for children with goodies and baddies but children know that witches and fairies do not exist; stepmothers on the other hand are very real. In real life children are aban-doned and abused by their fathers and stepfathers far more frequently than they are by women, but the wicked stepfather rarely features. By projecting all of their bad feelings onto the wicked stepmother, a child can maintain the fiction that their real mother and father is nothing but 'good'.

The typical fairy tale splitting of the mother into a good (usually dead) mother and an evil stepmother serves the child well . . . the fantasy of the wicked stepmother not only preserves the good mother intact, it also prevents having to feel guilty about one's angry thoughts and wishes about her – a guilt which would seriously interfere with the good relation to Mother.

Bruno Bettelheim, *The Uses of Enchantment –*
The Meaning and Importance of Fairy Tales

VANITY FAIR

Becky Sharp in *Vanity Fair*. She's clever, charming, calculating, charismatic and ruthless with an inner drive to survive. You certainly wouldn't want to be on the wrong side of her. As a penniless orphan she survives by her wits, manipulating the wealthy around her. She rejects traditional female attributes, showing little genuine affection for her own son, yet has the courage and the sharpness of mind to extricate both herself and her friend Amelia Sedley from the invading French and escape back to England. For those who resent strong women she is a bitch, but she is one of the most exciting and realistic female role models ever depicted in fiction and one Dorothy Parker admired enough to emulate.

When the parties were over, and the carriages had rolled away, the insatiable Miss Crawley would say, 'Come to my dressing room, Becky, and let us abuse the company', which between them this pair of friends did perfectly. Old Sir Huddleston wheezed a great deal at dinner; Sir Giles

Wapshot had a particularly noisy manner at imbibing his soup, and her ladyship a wink of the left eye; all of which Becky caricatured to admiration; as well as the particulars of the night's conversation; the politics; the war; the quarter-sessions; the famous run with the H.H., and those heavy and dreary themes, about which country gentlemen converse. As for the Misses Wapshot's toilettes and Lady Fuddleston's famous yellow hat, Miss Sharp tore them to tatters, to the infinite amusement of her audience'

From *Vanity Fair* by William Makepeace Thackery

JANE AUSTEN

Jane Austen's novels are full of entertaining bitches. Mrs Norris never fails to remind her niece Fanny that she is the poor relation in *Mansfield Park*. At the beginning of *Sense and Sensibility* Fanny Dashwood persuades her husband to reduce the income of his sisters Elinor and Marianne after their father's death; and the Bingley sisters in *Pride and Prejudice* have little to recommend them. But it is in *Emma*, the heroine whom according to Austen, 'no one but myself will much like,' that we have a masterpiece of a character. She's spoilt, manipulative and calculating. She's horrid to Miss Bates (see extract on page 19 of this section), takes on Harriet Smith as a friend and seeking to 'improve' her, persuades her not to marry the farmer she loves, for he is, Emma considers, beneath her. But Emma is not the stereotypical nasty bitch of fairy tales. She is clever and kind and that genuine mix of good and bad that is all women.

REBECCA

Mrs Danvers in Daphne du Maurier's *Rebecca* for preserving Rebecca's memory and being the grand mistress of the bitchy look. She stares at the second Mrs de Winter creepily, and just drops in the odd comment to make her feel small. 'Sometimes I wonder if she comes back here to Manderlay and watches you and Mr de Winter together,' she whispers as she shows her around Rebecca's quarters in the west wing. She sets her up for a fall at the fancy dress ball in much the same way as bitchy teenage girls do. Mrs Danvers suggests that she copies the costume in one of the portraits hanging in the hall, but fails to tell her that Rebecca did the very same thing for their last fancy dress party. As she descends to the party hoping to excite Max with her moment of glory, there is a hush of horrified silence and Max sends her back upstairs to change.

> I turned and ran blindly through the archway to the corridors beyond . . . Tears blinded my eyes. I did not know what was happening . . . I looked about me stunned and stupid like a haunted thing. Then I saw that the door leading to the west wing was open wide and that someone was standing there. It was Mrs Danvers. I shall never forget the expression on her face, loathsome, triumphant. The face of an exulting devil. She stood there, smiling at me.

Mrs Danvers' devotion to the cruel, charismatic, glamorous and audacious Rebecca knows no bounds. She even encourages the second Mrs de Winter to kill herself.

'Don't be afraid,' says Mrs Danvers, 'I won't push you . . .

you can jump of your own accord . . . you're not happy. Mr de Winter doesn't love you . . . why don't you jump now and have done with it? Then you won't be unhappy anymore.'

THE GROUP

Eight close friends and Vassar graduates gather together for Kay's wedding at the start of Mary McCarthy's *The Group*. Kay was the beautiful leader of the gang, but it is hard-nosed Norine who embarks on an affair with Kay's husband Harold and then colludes with him to have the perfectly sane Kay committed to a mental hospital. Five years later, Norine, now a young mother married to a wealthy banker, manages to make Priss who is married to a paediatrician, feel a great deal poorer and inadequate about her own mothering when she bumps into her in Central Park.

'She knows *you* very well,' observed Polly.

'Hey,' he said. 'That isn't like you Poll. You sound catty, like other women.'

'I am like other women.'

'No,' he shook his head, 'You're not. You're like a girl in a story book.'

Mary McCarthy on Lillian Hellman: Every word she writes is a lie, including 'and' and 'the'.

MACBETH

Lady Macbeth, the fourth witch who renounces the 'good' girl image of womanhood for ambition with 'Unsex me here, and fill me from Crowne to the Toe, top-full of direst Cruelty'. It is Lady Macbeth who encourages her husband to kill the king, Duncan. Yet as the drama unfolds, it is Macbeth who becomes stronger and more murderous, while his wife is plagued by the guilt over what they have done.

A THOUSAND ACRES

Rose in A *Thousand Acres* by Jane Smiley. Both Rose and her sister Ginny are classic, long-suffering women who looked after their abusive father and their younger sister Caroline after their mother died young. Caroline escaped small town life to become a lawyer but Rose and Ginny still live on the Iowan farm and cook their father's meals, pandering to his every whim. Rose is married to a violent man, has two daughters and has had breast cancer. Ginny has had five miscarriages and desperately wants children. All that self-sacrifice has to erupt somewhere, as the family falls out and squabbles over the inheritance of the farm in this modern retelling of the *King Lear* story. When Ginny falls in love with Jess Clark and Rose steals him from her because she cannot allow her sister happiness when she can't have it herself, it's the last straw for Ginny. Such is her anger and sense of betrayal that she tries to poison her sister, but fails. Then when Rose dies of secondary cancer, Ginny inherits guardianship of her nieces.

Anger itself reminds me of Rose, but so do most of the women I see on the street, who wear dresses she would have liked, ride children on their hips with the swaying grace that she had, raise their voices wishfully, knowingly, indignantly, ruefully, ironically, affectionately, candidly and even wrongly. Rose left me a riddle I haven't solved, of how we judge those who have hurt us when they have shown no remorse or even understanding.

THE EUSTACE DIAMONDS

Lady Eustace in *The Eustace Diamonds* by Anthony Trollope. Lizzie Eustace marries for money and soon becomes a widow at the age of twenty, inheriting the family estate and the valuable family diamond necklace, which she refuses to give back. She is one of the most entertaining and amoral characters to be found in any novel and Trollope's hilarious, bitchy description of her looks and 'dangerous', seductive, man-eating character deserves to be quoted in full.

It must be understood in the first place that she was very lovely: much more so indeed, now than when she had fascinated Sir Florian. She was small, but taller than she looked to be, for her form was perfectly symmetrical. Her feet and hands might have been taken as models by a sculptor. Her figure was lithe, and soft, and slim and slender. If it had a fault it was this, that it had in it too much of movement. There were some who said that she was almost snake-like in her rapid bendings and the almost too easy gestures of her body; for she was much given to action and to the expression of her thought by the motion on her limbs. She might certainly have made her way as an actress, had fortune called upon her to earn her bread in that fashion. And her voice would have suited the stage. It was powerful when she called upon it for power; but, at the same time, flexible and capable of much pretence at feeling. She could bring it to a whisper that would almost melt your heart with tenderness, as she had melted Sir Florian's, when she sat near to him reading poetry; and then she could raise it to a pitch of indignant wrath befitting a Lady Macbeth when her husband ventured to rebuke her. And her ear was quite correct in modulating these tones. She knew – and it must have been by instinct, for her culture in such matters was small – how to use her voice so that neither its tenderness nor its wrath should be misapplied. There were pieces in verse that she could read, things not wondrously good in themselves, so that she would ravish you; and she would so look at you as she did it that you would hardly dare either to avert your eyes or to return her gaze. Sir Florian had not known whether to do the one thing or the other, and had therefore seized her in his arms. Her face was oval – somewhat longer than an oval – with little in it, perhaps nothing in it, of that brilliancy of colour which we call complexion. And yet the shades of her countenance were ever changing between the softest and most transparent white and the richest mellowest shades of brown. It was only when she simulated anger – she was almost incapable of real anger – that she would succeed in calling the thinnest streak of pink from her heart, to show that there was blood running in her veins. Her hair, which was nearly black, but in truth was more of softness and of lustre than ever belong to hair that is really black, she wore bound tight round her perfect forehead, with one long lovelock hanging over her shoulder.

The form of her head was so good that she could dare to carry it without a chignon or any adventurous adjuncts from an artists' shop. Very bitter was she in consequence when speaking of the head-gear of other women. Her chin was perfect in its round – not over long, as is the case with so many such faces, utterly spoiling the sym-metry of the countenance. But it lacked a dimple and therefore lacked feminine tenderness. Her mouth was perhaps faulty in being too small, or, at least her lips were too thin. There was wanting from the mouth that expres-sion of eager-speaking truthfulness which full lips will often convey. Her teeth were without flaw or blemish, even, small, white and delicate; but perhaps they were shown too often. Her nose was small, but struck many as the prettiest feature of her face, so exquisite was the moulding of it, and so eloquent and so graceful the slight inflations of the transparent nostrils. Her eyes, in which she herself thought that the lustre of her beauty lay, were blue and clear, bright as cerulean waters. They were long, large eyes, but very dangerous. To those who knew how to read a face, there was a danger plainly written in them. Poor Sir Florian had not known. But in truth the charm of her face did not lie in her eyes. This was felt by many ever who could not read the book fluently. They were too expressive, too loud in their demands for attention and they lacked tenderness. How few there are among women, few perhaps also among men, who know that the sweetest, softest, tenderest, truest eyes which a woman can carry in her head are green in colour. Lizzie's eyes were not tender, neither were they true. But they were

surmounted by the most wonderfully pencilled eyebrows
that ever nature unassisted planted on a woman's face.

From *The Eustace Diamonds*

THE LIFE AND LOVES OF A SHE-DEVIL

Ruth in *The Life and Loves of a She Devil* by Fay Weldon brings
every wronged woman's deepest fantasies of revenge to life.
Ruth is a large woman with three hairy moles on her chin and
two small children. When her accountant husband runs off
with childless, best-selling romantic novelist Mary Fisher, Ruth
plots a series of evermore audacious deeds to bring them both
to their knees. She sets the house on fire, dumps the children
on their father, goes to work at an old people's home and gets
Mary's incontinent mother expelled so that she has to live
with them too. Then she starts shifting money around, builds
up her own business, gets wealthy and has her husband imprisoned for fraud during which time she begins to work on
improving her image cosmetically. As Mary Fisher's success
and self-esteem plummets; Ruth's soars.

I thought I was a good wife tried temporarily and understandably beyond endurance, but no. He says I am a
she-devil. I expect he is right. In fact, since he does so well
in the world and I do so badly, I really must assume he is
right. I am a she-devil. But this is wonderful! This is exhilarating! If you are a she-devil the mind clears at once. The
spirits rise. There is no shame, no guilt, no dreary striving to
be good. There is only in the end what you *want*. And I can
take what I want. I am a she-devil . . . peel away the wife,
the mother, find the woman and there the she-devil is.

THE FIRST WIVES CLUB

Annie, Elise and Brenda in *The First Wives Club* by Olivia Goldsmith. Goldsmith felt a deep sense of injustice when she went through an acrimonious divorce. The three feisty characters in her best-selling first novel band together to bring down the weak and cruel husbands who have traded them in like used cars for younger 'trophy' models. The shoutline for the book when it was first published in America was 'Don't get angry, get even.' Ivana Trump, who plays herself in the film version made in 1996 says 'Ladies, you have to be strong and independent, and remember, don't get mad, get everything.'

I was working on *Style* magazine when I wrote my first book and the editor there was a man and the bitchiest person in the world. His speciality was to do down anything I was wearing. I remember coming into work in a new pair of shoes once and he said, 'They're from M&S, aren't they? My wife tried them on, they looked cheap and nasty on her . . . but they look great on you!' Then when my first novel was published I discovered that my colleagues used to ring each other up and read each other the sex scenes and laugh like drains. One woman said, 'Oh Wendy, you've finished your book, it must be like having done a really big poo.' I discovered subsequently that she really wanted to write a book herself. Honestly, people are so jealous, they took the piss out of me but I had the last laugh. I got out.

Wendy Holden

George Bernard Shaw once sent two tickets to the opening night of one of his plays to Winston Churchill with the note, 'Bring a friend, if you have one.' Churchill returned the tickets and excused himself with the note 'Please send me two tickets for the next night, if there is one.'

How to Be a Better Bitch

Bitching is part of life. It's never going to go away and nor should it. It's hugely enjoyable banter, thrilling and liberating in its recklessness and an important cathartic release when life brings us down. We do it when we feel envious of others and can't bear the idea of them getting ahead. We do it when we feel trapped by conventional notions of what it is to be female – always kind, selfless, giving, perfect. We bitch about friends when we're pissed off because we find it hard to confront them openly and sometimes that's a good thing, better than being cruel or losing a friend for good. We bitch because the world of good manners where people behave with dignity and generosity is disappearing. And we bitch because so much of our culture is bitchy or revelatory, and entertainment like *Big Brother* revels in public humiliation.

There are times when it is just fine to be the bitch but first you have to acknowledge that you are one. There is a bitch inside each one of us, an inner Imelda Marcos just busting to get out, but few of us care to admit that. Women bitch a great deal because of the pressures associated with their gender. We learn the art at school and go on to excel at it. But it is only when we are conscious of our own strengths and weaknesses, including our ability to be cruel, that we are able to control that weapon of aggression and not use it inappropriately. With a greater sense of self, rooted in our genuine talents and attributes, we find the courage to be that strong bitch who inspires others – rather than that weak bitch who needs to put others down in order to feel stronger.

There are times when it is appropriate to be a bitch and times when it most definitely isn't. The important thing is to be able to recognise the difference between the two. It's fine to bitch about life to others when you're having a bad day or when you're made to feel powerless or inept by sadists in authority – patronising bosses, gynaecologists or health visitors. Its essential to bitch about lovers and husbands (both current and exes) when they're giving you a hard time. When married middle-aged men come on a bit strong, 'Say things like "I didn't know men went straight from puberty to adultery",' suggests novelist Kathy Lette, 'anything to put them off their clichéd course.' Bitching about members of the family with other family members or friends is acceptable because they will inevitably all be bitching about you too. It's crucial as a means of bonding and understanding mutual friends provided that you're not putting them down. And it's great fun to bitch about celebrities – that's part of their point.

But you enter dangerous waters if you extend your bitching panache to territories where you are liable to be labelled as 'the Bitch'. Don't bitch about your ex to your children. He's their dad and the fight is yours not theirs. One woman I heard of got her daughter to switch her ex-husband's SIM card for a blank one. She may have had good cause to be this vindictive but it was inappropriate to involve a child in her battle. Don't bitch in front of or directly at anybody under the age of about nineteen. It sets a bad example and can leave permanent scars. It's an abuse of your authority as a 'mature' person. Consider the spite of the woman who said to a friend's twelve-year-old daughter, 'You know, braces would make such a difference to your smile,' or the middle-aged successful academic, who, on hearing that a close friend's daughter had won a scholarship to Cambridge said, 'Did your parents know the admissions tutor?' Never bitch about your children's friends or their families at the school gate (it will get passed on) or in front of them. It will only make your child feel acutely embarrassed and uncomfortable and is likely to be repeated. We had a nickname for the father of a girl in my daughter's class at primary school – Laughing Joe. When I spotted him walking one day while I was in the car with another of my daughter's friends, and said, 'Oh look, there's Laughing Joe,' it got back to his daughter within hours of them returning to school and caused great embarrassment.

Not everybody in this world is likeable and there are people in this world that just aren't worth wasting bitching effort on. Save all of your best and most humorous comments for your equals – on friends you love the most who are strong enough to take it and bat back wit, or for those weak bitches who feel the need to put other women down and deserve to get as good as they give. Top quality bitching involves a high level of subtlety. Firstly you need to be funny. 'Just to complain is fantastically unattractive,' says agony aunt Virginia Ironside. 'It's not about being horrid and it isn't bitching unless it's funny and amusing.' If you're bitching about someone behind their back you want to seduce the person you are talking to with humour. If they laugh, they are less likely to think you're being a bitch. If you're lobbing a direct hit at someone, the barbed insult disguised as a joke will fall softly like a veil rather than provoking them to counter-attack and, who knows, they might even laugh. Secondly, it is important that any insult is delivered at such an acute angle, with so much top-spin that, should the recipient just happen to overhear, they would almost miss it. You part amicably before they stop to consider the significance of that last statement. By the time they realise that they have actually been insulted, you're miles away escaping retribution, you've doubly insulted them because they now feel really stupid because they didn't get it immediately and most importantly you've had the last word.

Masking your words with much more positive body language is a core component of successful bitching. We build rapport with others by mirroring their posture and voice tone and giving the impression that we are in sync. If our words suggest otherwise but are masked by a smile, it is harder for the recipient to believe that you just said that, or meant that aggressively. It's important to stay calm and in control when you sting. If you get angry or upset you lose control and the danger of that is that you slip out of subtle bitchery into rude country. If you stay calm and cool, it's very hard for others to come back at you and if they accuse you of being a bitch you can just chuck out 'So?' or 'Whatever'. It's important to give the impression that you really don't care what others think of you, even though you do.

Put yourself down along with everybody else. 'They used to photograph Shirley Temple through gauze,' said Tallulah Bankhead. 'They should photograph me through linoleum.'

Katharine Hepburn had it in for Shirley Temple as well. 'Acting is the most minor of gifts. After all Shirley Temple could do it when she was four.'

Master the art of damning praise. I love to play tennis and go occasionally on a girls' weekend to a tennis centre. I am without a doubt the worst player of the gang, but whenever I say so, everybody denies this and offers me plenty of sisterly encouragement. On our way home one Sunday evening, another woman was encouraging me to come and play with them at the local tennis club. I said I didn't think I was good enough. 'Oh, there's loads of women there who are worse than you are,' another woman piped up and the truth was finally out. I laughed the loudest. It's a fabulous model that can be adapted to any circumstance. When someone keeps putting themselves down and actually you just wish they'd stop hog-ging the limelight just say, 'There are plenty of people fatter/uglier/poorer/bitchier than you are' and you are also making a valid point. The grass is always greener. There are plenty of people out there worse off than you.

Agree with people. When people are being irritating, iden-tify what it is that needs attention and then attack under the veil of complicit criticism whenever they come close to criti-cising others for the same thing. A friend is training to be a teacher and another woman on the course kept interrupting the teacher-trainer because her opinions and observations were, of course, so much more important than anybody else's. After several days of this the colleague interrupted once again with 'Well you can't have all the children shouting out at the same time . . .' and the teacher agreed, 'Yes, it is very irritating when people keep on interrupting . . .' As soon as the person strays anywhere near their own weaknesses in their criticisms of others, you agree, replace their criticisms with yours and hit back.

It's important to preface any conversation with someone that's about to turn into a bitch with something entirely positive about them. 'Don't get me wrong, I really like her/she's one of my best friends/she has masses of good qualities . . . but . . .' Then you can launch into an unkind rant with a completely clear conscience and return to those positive aspects if the other person criticises you for being too harsh. 'I do hope that when people bitch about me,' says Virginia Ironside, 'they do the same thing. I want that preamble.'

When any woman feels intimidated or undermined in an overtly masculine environment bitching is a crucial means of defence, provided it's done with a sweet smile and just that little hint of flirtation so that men are confused. Use verbal retorts that might make them question their assumptions. Ex-city banker Helena Frith Powell heard two glittering examples of Mae West-style wit. When a female colleague received an email with a picture of the sender's (male) genitals attached she pinged back the reply, 'Looks like a penis, only smaller.' Another colleague when invited to join a 'bonding' trip to a strip club replied, 'No thanks, but how are your daughters getting on there?' We are grand mistresses in the art of verbal put-down and we should use it to our advantage under threat. We do not have to pander permanently to the 'good' girl notion, where we are always kind, considerate to the needs of others, caring and sharing. Sometimes it does us no harm to be Cruella De Vil.

But there are also some definite 'Don'ts' which betray rules of good friendship. If someone tells you something derogatory about a friend, never pass it on. Don't forward critical emails either. Never rank your friends, that's childish too. The writer Elizabeth Noble was in a bar with a group of girlfriends when one of them revealed that she and her boyfriend had been playing a game where he ranked her friends according to sexual attractiveness on a scale of 1–10. Big mistake. Why say this? Conversations between lovers should be private. 'I looked a bit worried about this,' said Elizabeth, 'but then my friend said I shouldn't worry because her boyfriend had thought I was a bit round but that I would be great fun in bed.' Then another friend said, 'So, what did he say about me?' The reply was stinging, 'Oh no, we didn't talk about you.'

If someone else is being bitchy to you and you can't think of a quick suitable response, then sometimes the best way to diminish their sting is simply to agree with them. Take a leaf out of prime bitch Bette Davis's book: 'I played three roles on the screen that Tallulah Bankhead had created on stage and then in *All About Eve* my character was said to have been inspired by her. I'd never met her,' she told biographer Charlotte Chandler. 'One evening at a party I saw her stalking menacingly across the room right toward me. She was definitely not sober and she was obviously looking for a quarrel. She said "Dah-ling – You've managed to play my best parts, but not as well as I did." I wasn't in the mood to oblige her with an off-stage confrontation. So I simply responded, "Miss Bankhead – I agree with you *absolutely*." That took the wind out of her sails and she didn't have anywhere to go with it, so she retired from the scene.'

'We survive our critics by knowing that their agendas have

little to do with us.' Wise words from a surprising source I say, bitchily perhaps. Sarah, Duchess of York was famously nick-named the Duchess of Pork by a particular newspaper editor. When she found herself sitting next to him at a dinner years later she realised that he had in fact just been doing his job and that he didn't have anything personal against her. It can be hard not to take things personally when someone else is bitch-ing about you, but often their aggression isn't really about you, it's just that you happen to be in the right spot at the wrong time, when that person feels like lashing out to make them-selves feel stronger or more secure. Latch onto their weaknesses at all times to feel stronger and remember the words of Oscar Wilde: 'There is only one thing in life worse than being talked about and that is not being talked about.'

As women grow older they learn to care less about what others think of them. We put ourselves first once our children are independent enough to do things for themselves. We wear what we want when a sexualised appearance matters less. We say what we really think about things, able to rage against injustice, and we do what we want, rather than what others want us to do. If we could adopt just some of this stronger sense of self at an earlier age, life would be rich enough to be more forgiving of other women. Being more aware of the female stereotypes that constrain us is a good place to start. If we per-petuate the negative patriarchal view that women fall into stereotypes – the 'bimbo', the 'airhead', the 'good' mother or the 'hard-nosed bitch', rather than individuals with a range of emotions typical to all human beings we divide rather than unite, judging others for not living up to these false illusions of how women should be. We perpetuate the myth that women's friendships are plagued by deceit and betrayal, when the vast majority of women say that incidences of these are rare, that their friendships with women are the most nourishing and valuable relationships they have ever known. We endorse the myth that men are less capable of caring for children or doing housework by presuming that only women can do it and we take on far more social and familial responsibilities as working women than we can manage. By finding the courage to bust out of these stereotypes, we find the freedom to be less con-formist and achieve more as individuals. True leaders and motivators are charismatic, not bitches. They draw others in to help them achieve something and their charismatic strength is infectious, able to lift and inspire others – public speakers and performers with the ability to play an audience, teachers who can control a class, managers who unite people behind them as a team and politicians who get respect by hitting upon a common truth.

When we compete with each for male attention, for romance or for work by putting each other down, we fail to see the bigger picture where the stakes against all women are high. Women's bodies are degraded on every advertising hoarding and magazine. Women earn less than men in equivalent jobs (if they can get them) and still bear the brunt of poverty, vio-lence, sexual abuse, and carry the burden of caring for family and our most vulnerable people in society. We ought to bitch about that a great deal more, but the chances of changing any-thing to make society fairer and safer for women seem so remote that we bitch (moan) about it to each other or bitch about (put down) each other instead. Instead of hitting out at injustice, we hit out at each other and we believe that we are somehow the problem. The good life is out there for us to grab if we just believe in ourselves, work at our body image and work with the status quo rather than questioning it. If we fail, now that girls can 'have it all', we have only ourselves to blame. And we do. A burgeoning self-help market tells us how to look into ourselves to sort the problem.

True empathy and kindness come from a sense of security, not from the false construct of female selflessness. Women have a unique bond. They are acutely sensitive to the inner emotional landscape of people and have profound strengths and abilities when it comes to helping and improving the lives of others. But only when that comes from a position of individual strength and a sense of self-fulfilment, for without that resentment of others flourishes. We have a right to put ourselves and our own needs first and not wait until we are in our fifties to begin to pursue our dreams.

In the end the key to our own happiness lies within ourselves. If we decide to be happy enough with the way we look; the appearance of others matters less. If we focus on the many strengths and assets that we have; there is less to envy in other women. If we are honest about what we want from life; we are more likely to meet those aspirations and less likely to feel the need to pass a moral judgment on those who pursue a different path. We can simply decide to be the mothers we are, talented in some departments, crap in others. That's how we can become the strong type of 'bitch' who fulfils her potential and her dreams and feels genuinely good about herself, rather than the scheming, manipulative, envious type of 'bitch' who needs to damn other women in order to make herself feel more powerful. Then when that strong 'bitch' feels that burning desire for a really good bitching session with a good friend, she has many more resources at her disposal to do it well.

I've learned that no matter what happens, or how bad it seems today, life does go on and it will be better tomorrow. I've learned you can tell a lot about a person by the way s/he handles three things: a rainy day, lost luggage and tangled Christmas tree lights. I've learned that regardless of your relationship with your parents you will miss them when they're gone from your life. I've learned that 'making a living' is not the same as making a 'life'. I've learned that life sometimes gives you a second chance. I've learned that you shouldn't go through life with a catcher's mitt on both hands; you need to be able to throw some things back. I've learned that when I decide something with an open heart I've usually made the right decision. I've learned that even when I have pains I don't have to be one. I've learned that every day you should reach out and touch someone. People love a warm hug or just a friendly tap on the back. I've learned that I've still got a lot to learn. I've learned that people will forget what you said, people will forget what you did, but people will never forget how you made them feel.

**Maya Angelou on her 70th birthday
on the *Oprah Winfrey Show***

Acknowledgements

My heartfelt thanks go to all those wonderful bitches who have not recoiled at the subject matter and have shared their views with me. I would like to thank Terri Apter, Maryann Barlow, Hillary Brittain, Diana Boxer, Elizabeth Buchan, Jerome Burne, Anne Campbell, Margaret Clark, Amanda Craig, Marcelle D'Argy Smith, Cecilia Darker, Lennie Goodings, Marjorie Harness Goodwin, Judy Hamilton, Michele Hanson, Louette Harding, Wendy Holden, Jennifer Howell, Virginia Ironside, Adrienne Katz, Beeban Kidron, Tamsin Kitson, Kevin Kniffin, Kathy Lette, Carrie Longton, Elizabeth Mapstone, Vanessa Neuling, Elizabeth Nobel, Hazel Norbury, Stephanie Lawler, Lee Oggier, Susie Orbach, Allison Pearson, Justine Picardie, Gill Pyrah, Mary Robey, Felicity Rubinstein, Elizabeth Sigmund, Natalie Signeux, Susie Silvey, Helen Simpson, Donna Williams, Rosalind Wiseman, Eleanor Wyld, Grace Wyld. Your views have helped shape this book and I am deeply grateful for your contributions.

The bitch in me would also like to list the many women I approached who refused help but that's unnecessarily divisive . . .

All of the names of young people under the age of eighteen have been changed to protect their identities. Their locations have also been changed. But you all know who you are. Thank you for being so honest and outspoken and I hope this book helps you all to be stronger, and consequently kinder to each other.

As always, my deepest thanks go to my daughters and their father Christoph for their love and support.

~

I am deeply grateful to Amanda Craig for her piece on Top Teen reading and to Michele Hanson for her piece on gossip. Copyright in both resides with the authors. I am grateful to Copper Canyon Press for permission to reproduce 'Bitch' by Carolyn Kizer. Thanks to Bloomsbury for permission to quote from *Cat's Eye* by Margaret Atwood. Thanks to Century for permission to quote from *Bette and Joan: The Divine Feud* by Shaun Considine.

Sources

Apter, Terri *You Don't Really Know Me* (Norton 2004)

—— *The Myth of Maturity* (Norton 2001)

Bettelheim Bruno *The Uses of Enchantment* (Vintage 1989)

Besag, Valerie E. *Understanding Girls' Friendships, Fights and Feuds* (Open University Press 2006)

Bowman, Grace *A Shape of My Own* (Viking, 2006)

Brown, Lyn Mikel *Girlfighting* (New York University Press 2003)

—— *Raising Their Voices* (Harvard 1998)

—— and Gilligan, Carol *Meeting at the Crossroads* (Harvard 1992)

Campbell, Anne 'Female Competition: Causes, Constraints, Content and Contexts' (*Journal of Sex Research* Feb 2004)

—— *Staying Alive: Evolution, Culture and Women's Intra-sexual Aggression* (University of Durham, 2005)

Chandler, Charlotte *The Girl Who Walked Home Alone* (Simon & Schuster 2006)

Chesler, Phyllis *Woman's Inhumanity to Woman* (Plume 2003)

Coates, Jennifer (ed.) *Language and Gender* (Blackwell 1998)

Considine, Shaun *Bette and Joan: The Divine Feud* (Time Warner Books 1989)

Crewe, Candida *Eating Myself* (Bloomsbury 2006)

Eder, Donna *School Talk: Gender and Adolescent Culture* (Rutgers University Press 2003)

Fox, Kate 'Evolution, Alienation and Gossip' (www.sirc.org/publik/gossip.shtml 2005)

Garbarino, James *And Words Can Hurt Forever* (Free Press 2002)

Goleman, Daniel *Social Intelligence: The New Science of Human Relationships* (Hutchinson 2006)

Goodwin, Marjorie Harness *The Hidden Life of Girls* (Blackwell Publishing 2006)

Jahme, Carole *Beauty and the Beasts: Woman, Ape and Evolution* (Soho Press 2001)

Kniffin, Kevin M. and Wilson, David Sloan 'Utilities of Gossip across Organizational Levels' (*Human Nature* Vol 16, Number 3)

Kobak, Stu *The Bitch Brigade* (www.filmsondisc.com)

Louvish, Simon *Mae West: It Ain't No Sin* (Faber 2005)

Meade, Marion *Dorothy Parker: What Fresh Hell is This* (Penguin 1989)

Mooney, Nan *I Can't Believe She Did That!* (St Martin's Press 2005)

Orbach, Susie and Luise Eichenbaum *Between Women* (Arrow 1987)

Quinlan, David *Wicked Women of the Screen* (St Martins Press 1989)

Simmons, Rachel *Odd Girl Out: The Hidden Culture of Aggression in Girls* (Harcourt 2002)

Smuts, Barbara 'Sexual Competition and Mate Choice in Primate Societies' edited by B.B. Smuts, D.L. Cheney, R.M. Seyfrath, R.W. Wrangham, T.T. Struhsaker (University of Chicago Press, 1987)

Tannen, Deborah *You Just Don't Understand* (Virago 1990)

Tanenbaum, Leora *Slut! Growing up Female with a Bad Reputation* (Seven Stories Press 1999)

—— *Catfight* (Perennial 2003)

Thompson, Michael and O'Neil, Grace, Catherine with Laurence J. Cohen *Best Friend, Worst Enemies: Children's Friendships, Popularity and Social Cruelty* (Michael Joseph 2001)

Weldon, Fay *What Makes Women Happy* (Fourth Estate 2006)

Wiseman, Rosalind *Queen Bees and Wannabes* (Piatkus 2002)

Wurtzel, Elizabeth *Bitch* (Quartet 1998)

www.askmen.com

www.bbc.co.uk/weakestlink

www.blogcritics.org
www.digitalspy.co.uk
www.filmsite.org
www.imdb.com
www.popdirt.com

TURN OVER
THIS BOOK
TO FIND
OUT HOW
FROM LITTLE
BITCHES,
BIG BITCHES
GROW . . .

NOW TURN OVER THIS BOOK TO FIND OUT HOW THE BIG BITCHES DO IT . . .

The Big
Fat Bitch
Book

The Big
Fat Bitch
Book
for Girls

KATE FIGES

virago

VIRAGO

First published in Great Britain in 2007 by Virago Press

A CIP catalogue record for this book
is available from the British Library.

ISBN 978-1-84408-295-7

Papers used by Virago are natural, recyclable products made
from wood grown in sustainable forests and certified in accordance
with the rules of the Forest Stewardship Council.

Typeset in Goudy by M Rules
Printed and bound in Great Britain by
Clays Ltd, St Ives plc

Virago Press
An imprint of
Little, Brown Book Group
Brettenham House
Lancaster Place
London WC2E 7EN

A Member of the Hachette Livre Group of Companies

www.virago.co.uk

I dedicate this book to the person who
let their dog shit on my doorstep . . .

Contents

Introduction

A couple of pictures of you in a cheap little outfit get into the papers and now you're the new me? You reckon you're the new Queen of Glamour because you were snapped falling out of a club with a couple of belts strapped round those saggy boobs. Not exactly pert are you?

Jordan to Jodie Marsh

They are not sagging, love – they're real. Just because they don't touch my chin and they're not rock-hard, doesn't mean they are saggy and horrible.

Jodie Marsh to Jordan

~

Bitching can be the best fun ever. When girls get together for girltalk about life, love and other people, we couldn't feel closer or laugh louder. It's a particularly delicious female pleasure. Few things are more interesting than other people and their weird quirks or the human failings we're all vulnerable to. We love to analyse other people's motives and behaviour. We define what's in or out style-wise and what's morally acceptable or unacceptable by gossiping about how other people look or behave. We support each other through the maze of problems that we face as girls, with invaluable advice about school, friendship difficulties, periods, parents, boys and personal disappointments – but that's almost impossible without talking about other people. All of us, however young or old, bitch to unwind and let off steam; it's completely normal. 'I'm sorry but there's no way that no girl hasn't bitched about anyone,' says fifteen-year-old Anna from Durham. 'Lads even bitch. You have to have a bitch because it gets everything off your chest.' We bitch to complain for there is a great deal to understand as we grow up. 'If you don't bitch you just feel like you're really tied up with not telling anyone anything,' said another fifteen-year-old from London. Girls bitch about each other's appearance, how much money they haven't got, teachers and who does what with boys. 'Anything can lead to bitching, even who has the nicest dining-room table,' said one thirteen-year-old. Another fifteen-year-old from a different school points out the paradox. 'The only way to have a conversation and not bitch is to keep your mouth shut.'

Bitching can be wonderfully positive and good for us. *The Big Fat Bitch Book* will explain why girls are particularly good at bitching and put you in touch with your inner bitch. For we all have one. But there is also a dark side to the intense intimacy of girlworld: the cruel put-downs made by the weak and insecure to make them seem more powerful and popular, the bitching which turns into a vicious and sustained form of bullying because adults fail to detect it. Often close friendship groups turn on one particular girl in their midst. They keep their target hanging on by a thread, including her in their plans just enough to make her believe she is a friend, but also excluding her or bitching about her the moment her back is turned. The occasional bitch, 'isn't bullying,' says Adrienne Katz of the children's charity Young Voice, 'but the drip, drip effect intended to bring you to a desperate state definitely is.'

When bitching becomes bullying girls pursue campaigns of evil looks, blanking, rumour spreading and ritual humiliation that few teachers and parents recognise or believe possible. And without acknowledgement from adults that girls can be this cruel, or having your complaints dismissed with 'ignore them, sticks and stones may break my bones but words will never hurt me', it's easy to believe as the victim that you are in fact to blame – if only I was thinner, prettier, more popular then maybe they'd stop picking on me. Bitch bullies whittle away your confidence and sense of self by continually making you feel as if you are to blame, and as lots of the girls who talk openly about bitching in this book will testify, it hurts – it really hurts.

The Big Fat Bitch Book will explain why we bitch and show you how to keep the cruelty within us all to a minimum. We bitch out of jealousy and envy of what others have. We bitch when we feel angry and powerless, competitive or bored. We bitch about others to focus the attention of our friends on their weaknesses so that they fail to notice our own failings. That's human, normal, nothing to be ashamed of, provided we are honest about our motives and nobody finds out. 'There's a big difference between bitching about something or someone and being a bitch,' says Lily, who is fifteen. 'A bitch is some-one who hurts people for the fun of it or to get her own way and leaves mangled bodies behind her. To bitch about someone because it's fun or because they're annoying you or everyone else is doing it too can be equally hurtful, but only if you find out about it – and it's the bitches who make sure you do.'

Growing up has never been easy but girls face far more contradictory pressures today than ever before. The emphasis on traditional feminine appearance, looking attractive, thin and 'girly' with short skirts and make-up is very strong within a highly charged sexual culture. You need money, a great deal of it, to achieve the aspired look and most of us just don't have it, particularly when we're young. Girls grow up feeling sexy, and just as interested in sex and becoming sexual beings as the boys, yet the prevailing moral code at school is that 'good' girls don't do sex and are bitched about as 'slags' if there is even a hint that they might do. Girls still grow up absorbing stereotypical notions of how girls should be – always kind not cruel, calm never angry, cooperative rather than selfish, supportive, caring and enabling of others rather than competitive. These are admirable characteristics, ones we should expect of everybody, but when girls feel they have to conform to these feminine stereotypes it's much harder for them also to exhibit ambition, drive, competitive spirit, even ruthlessness, all essential attributes for success in the wider world of work. You want to excel and get straight A's but you can't say so, for that would be bragging. So you pretend not to have done any work at all, or not to be too interested in school so as not to appear disloyal to your group of friends or uncool. You want to succeed in a particular field, but if doing so is going to make a friend feel uncomfortable about not knowing what she wants to be when she grows up, you swallow that ambition and feel unable to talk openly about it.

All too often girls, and women, bitch about others because they are envious of what they possess or have achieved but don't feel confident enough or sure of their ability to strive for those same goals. We bitch because we feel the things we really want seem scarce and beyond our grasp. We bitch because we feel vulnerable most of the time. We rarely feel entirely happy with the way we look, or the way we are treated and it is much easier to put down other women than to challenge the wider world that still sets different rules for boys and girls. We can't escape bitching. It's all around us now, in comedy programmes like *Little Britain* and *Friends*, reality shows such as *Big Brother* and even quizzes with Anne Robinson's *The Weakest Link*. Magazines such as *Heat* and *Sneak* trash celebrities for their sweat lines and cellulite. It has become so acceptable to say publicly what we think, even if it's rude, hurts or humiliates, that it can be hard for a girl to know where the lines of good etiquette and manners lie any more. With an understanding of bitching technique, you will begin to recognise whether your friends are bitching out of insecurity, sheer malice, or because they want to be firmer friends with you, and you will be able to give as good as you get.

There is a big difference between being the strong kind of successful, admired bitch who knows who she is and what she wants from life, able to challenge and show originality without caring (much) about what others think of her, and the weak bitch whom nobody much likes. The strong bitch feels enough self-confidence not to need to put others down; the weak kind of bitch excels at manipulating others, making them feel small so that she can feel more powerful. This book will show you how to be more of that first strong kind of bitch and genuinely popular. It will also show you how to limit the damage by shoring up your defences if you find yourself the target of a bitch bully campaign. For once trapped by this form of abuse, and it is abuse and should be labelled as such, a girl soon learns how to be the quiet accommodator, not wanting to say or do anything that could be laughed at or used against her. She loses self-respect when she learns to be loved on someone else's terms and that's a terrible model for adulthood. Real women, real bitches are better than that. Much better.

**Anne Robinson's Top Ten Intellectual Put-downs
on *The Weakest Link***

- 'I don't think you should be allowed to breed'
- 'Your mind will explode doing something it's not used to doing – thinking'
- 'Who here is the dog muck under the leather sandal?'
- 'You would be out of your depth in a car park puddle'
- 'You seem to have delusions of adequacy'
- 'Which of you got into the gene pool when the lifeguard wasn't watching?'
- 'Is there any beginning to your knowledge?'
- 'Perhaps the show should be called the *missing* link'
- 'You are not so much a has-been, but more like a definitely won't be'
- 'Who's broken out in a rash of ignorance?'

Girls and Boys Come Out to Play

You don't have to be Einstein to work out that boys and girls often behave in very different ways when they play and relate. That's where some of the roots of bitching lie. Boys like to charge around the playground in large amorphous groups kicking balls; girls play hopscotch, fantasy games, but mostly, from the age of eight or nine they like to sit in smaller, intimate huddles and gossip. Boys like playing competitive team games with clear rules and they tend to be much happier about being judged publicly with challenges and target setting – how many times can you kick that ball in the air without it touching the ground? Who can piss the furthest? Boys are also happy to acknowledge that there is a distinct hierarchy in their year group with a top dog who is likely to be sporty and tall or more mature than the others.

Girls like to be more cooperative when they play games. They like to give the impression that they are equals with their friends and competition undermines that, for someone invariably has to lose as well as win. So they take it in turns, like good girls are supposed to do, and then when they feel that competitive urge surface look for more underhand ways to win – rattling the skipping rope a girl is jumping over when they want a turn, queue-jumping or accusing others of being selfish/spoilt/too 'up themselves' or vain so that they can bring them back into line and therefore feel better about themselves, for girls who attempt to shine make others feel inadequate. Girls tend to compete less openly and honestly than boys over aspects of their personal appearance or social circumstances that are hard to change – clothes, material possessions, image, close friendships. They eye each other up, making a mental note about everything another girl says, wears or does in order to establish where she sits in an invisible social pecking order. 'Girls spend a lot of time assessing other people's activities, evaluating the social scene, who's in and who's out. They enjoy it,' Marjorie Harness Goodwin, American anthropologist and author of *The Hidden Life of Girls* explained to me, 'and bitching is a way of sanctioning girls who think they're better than the others. It can be anything – the way she walks down the street, or having something new, or her mother allowing her to do something that the others aren't allowed to do, which leads to jealousy.'

Girls also tend to form much more intimate and emotionally supportive relationships with each other than boys do, confiding secrets, fears and failings, discussing other mutual friends in their absence. This is valuable information in the wrong hands, when young people are still testing the boundaries of friendship and where true loyalty and betrayal lie. Once friends know each other's weaknesses they often unwittingly find ways to undermine each other, subtly . . . 'When you bitch to boys about girls it goes over their heads, they don't understand it,' says Juliet from Hastings, 'but with girls if you tell them something it goes into their brains and they think How can I use this? Who can I tell?'

Girls use bitching as a means of underhand competition, to get ahead, to show others they are in the know because it's an irresistible way to stir things up when they are bored or to forge friendships with others they would like to be closer to. They also use bitching as a weapon of aggression. Boys tend to lash out with their fists and get into fights when they get angry. The incident is more public, lanced by parents or teachers and usually quickly forgotten. Marjorie Harness Goodwin has studied the way that girls and boys play and believes there are marked differences in the way that each gender insults each other ritually. 'Boys can be very bitchy too, but what they say to each other is usually not true, and it's usually wind-ups about their mothers. Then they get competitive with each other about who can say the worst thing and it's usually much more jocular. But with girls, insults are almost always founded in truth and can be much more upsetting.' Girls know where to hit each other verbally so that it really hurts.

Girls rely that much more on their friendships for support and consequently really dislike doing anything that might mean risking losing a friendship for ever, like getting cross or irritated when friends are being annoying or inconsiderate. Even telling a friend that they have upset them can be difficult. They also don't want to create opportunities for others to bitch about them by creating a scene. So girls bitch about each other behind their backs as a means of preserving the status quo and not offending others.

Politics enters friendship at an early age as girls begin to share secrets and bond in intimate clusters, buying friends with gifts and party invitations. 'It used to be really peaceful at my primary school,' says Hannah, 'but then when we were ten and eleven the bullying started, like if you weren't into sports you just got bullied. One of my friends and a couple of others started this hate club against this weirdo because no one liked her, and nobody wanted to stand up for her because they were too scared they'd be the next victim. They did really sneaky things so that if she went to the teacher they would think it was nothing.'

As children begin to grow up through adolescence they embark upon a slow and inexorable path, separating from the security that comes from their families and they rely on their friends that much more for support. Consequently the prospect of losing that support is terrifying. They don't like to be the first to leave their gang of friends in case they get talked about, and saying anything negative about a mutual friend can be dangerous. 'Sometimes you're scared to say anything about anybody in case two people get together and talk about it, and if you do tell somebody something you never know whether or not they're going to tell somebody else and then it carries on through the group,' says Mandy from Newcastle. And if you do lose the support that comes from that group of friends, it can be hard to find it elsewhere because other groups have formed and nobody wants to be on their own. 'It can be hard if you have this friend that you don't really like,' says Olivia who is thirteen, 'because there are all these other groups and it isn't very easy to join them. All these groups are so separate.'

Cliques

Beware of the Plastics . . . They're team royalty.

Mean Girls

At the top of each year are the 'Princesses'. They all have lots of money and wear Louis Vuitton and have fake tans, pink mirrors and phones. They come to school dressed as if they're going to a wedding with diamondy earrings and they're like so *clean* you just want to ruffle their hair. We call them the 'Gucci princesses' or the 'orange' people because of their fake tans. We have a problem with 'orange' people because we think they should live a little. There's more to life than shopping and looking in a mirror.

Then below them are the Top Shop people. That's us. Well off but not too full of themselves. Below that are those who try to fit in with the other two groups but can't. They try too hard and anyway they don't have enough money. Then below that are the 'retards'. They're just different. They stick together but they don't dress or act like each other. They're sort of in their own world.

Sam and Claudia are fourteen and attend an independent girls' day school in London.

Cliques form in every secondary school and in every year group. They are an important part of growing up. When you find yourself penned together with so many other diverse types of people in large, dense schools, it's understandable that you should feel the need to form closer friendships with other people who you feel are of like mind. Grown-ups do exactly the same. Children unite around similar clothing, music tastes, leisure pursuits and use of language. They occupy the same territory at school, such as particular seats in the dining hall or the playground. They are usually racially homogenous and come from the same class or the same areas of their town or city and they often share similar aspirations.

Schools have become larger and more vibrant in their ethnic mix and what they teach offering a valuable education for life now that we thrive as a multicultural society. But as diversity, and therefore differences are highlighted, young people cluster together more in cliques according to their class and race to bolster their shaky and emerging sense of self as they start to grow up. Cliques are a bit like health insurance: they create a protective, invisible membrane, a bubble around each individual child, enabling them to explore further away from the safety of home with their gang of friends. Young people affirm that membrane constantly by touching each other, herding along the street in packs, texting and phoning each other, yelling at each other from different buses as they go home and ignoring all those who exist outside that membrane.

'We always stick up for each other and we're quite intimidating and loud. We don't care what people are saying about us,' says Juliet, who is fifteen and in a group of about twenty at a large comprehensive. 'All the other groups, they're nobodies to us. We're the most middle-class girls of our year, so we stick together. Our humour distinguishes us in that not many other people get it. We're sarcastic, very un-P.C. We call weirdos "kiddy fiddlers" and take the piss out of 'em. We're experienced as a group but not everyone has done everything. We don't go too far and we're not particularly rebellious. We also do our school work, which distinguishes us from some of the other groups who don't care and drop out and drink. There's also the really druggie group. I don't like them.'

Each year group has its hierarchy of cliques, which is eerily reflective of adult society. Popularity is the most valued currency, even if being popular doesn't necessarily mean being liked. The higher status 'popular' cliques tend to contain members with the most advanced social skills, the best looks, confident personalities and sporting talents and know very little about what goes on outside their group. 'There are two different popular groups at the top of our year,' says a fourteen-year-old girl from a single-sex school in Leeds, 'and they hang out with each other a lot but they also bitch about each other behind their backs. Some are a bit more sporty and some are into boys and make-up but they'll cross over quite a lot. Then you have people who are really, really nice as a rule but not so cool and they'll band together, and then underneath them you have little dots of groups. I know that the popular groups are definitely on top of me and if they decide to start a rumour about me or talk about me behind my back, people are going to believe them. People are scared of them because of what they can do to you.' And as with adult society, the top echelons of school society rarely recognise their privilege. They complain about being copied or how the lower orders try to get in with them but deny that they are bitches or refuse to recognise that bitchiness even exists with 'everyone sort of gets on with everyone else really'.

There are often several leaders providing different functions within each clique – the clown, the social motivator, the negotiator – and it is the leaders who tend to determine dress code, activities and attitudes. 'Sometimes there's just one person who is really bossy and people will do what they say because they're a bit scary,' says Sian, who is thirteen, 'and if she says she doesn't like somebody then everybody else in the group will agree with her because they don't want to lose the security that comes from being part of that group.' The more popular you are as a clique, the more people there are courting your friendship and with that comes additional anxieties – do they really like me or what my popularity can bring? The pressure to look the best and be the 'coolest' is even more intense and the prospect of being cast out even more terrifying, so they get bitchier. The borders of your bubble have to be controlled carefully in case anyone should challenge your position, your right to be within the bubble at all. 'Girls gain a lot of power by being able to reposition people,' says Marjorie Harness Goodwin. 'If someone's talked about behind her back then that justifies retribution and sometimes they will even fabricate people saying nasty things to gain new alliances.' By engaging in conflict as a group against others you maintain your entity, that invisible membrane that surrounds and protects you. Nobody is ever singled out as being responsible and feelings of guilt are diluted within the clique.

Adults are sometimes suspicious of adolescent cliques and teenagers rarely like to admit that they are part of one because the word has so many negative connotations. But teenagers are just young people with exactly the same social patterns and needs. Adults group together with people of like mind and join clubs with criteria for inclusion and therefore exclusion and plenty of adults crave the status that comes with being important, such as being invited to all the best parties. At work adults like to feel in the loop, included with privileged information. Teenagers spend more time with their friends than they do with anybody else, or than any other age group. Feeling contained and understood within a bubble of firm friendships is essential protection for teenagers as they grow up and learn from their mistakes. Cliques are generally good for teenage health, rather than damaging. There's strength in numbers. They dare to do things together that they would never dare do alone. It is loneliness, not feeling part of a group, ostracism and expulsion from that protective bubble, which causes the greatest distress, and sadly it tends to be the most powerful cliques of girls who pick on one of their members as a kind of sport.

The most heartbreaking interview I conducted for this book was with five eleven-year-old girls. They had been friends at primary school, they lived in close proximity to one another and moved up to the same secondary school together. The rest of their year group came from different primary schools so they were forced to stick together as a group rather than branch out and find new friends. Moving up to secondary school is stressful for many children. They move from being the oldest of the pack to the youngest, more is expected of them and they have lots of different teachers rather than one form tutor for everything. Within days of moving up to secondary school, this group of five girls began to fight and the four biggest turned on the smallest, Jane, and accused her of trying to steal away one of their friends from their primary school, flirting with a boy and being bossy. 'She gets on our nerves,' said Emma, the obvious leader of the gang. She did most of the talking and looked regularly to the other three for support against Jane. 'In class sometimes she like gives us dirty looks and we get fed up with it and sometimes when everyone's talking she comes a bit closer and starts talking about me and my sister behind my back and that's like really personal and she bosses us around and we don't want anyone telling us what to do. We'll say, "We're going to the youth workers" and she'll say, "No we're not we're going to the canteen" when we don't want to go to the canteen.'

Not long into the interview, Jane begins to cry and it's clear that she has been trying to reassert herself within the group. 'It's not that I don't want to go to the youth workers, it's just that I don't wanna be on my own because I worry that they'll talk about me.' When I pointed out to Emma, the leader, that it must be hurtful and that it's hard for one person to stand up for herself when four of your closest friends gang up against you, Emma threw the blame back on Jane. 'We feel that she's doing this herself, she's pushing away from us on purpose and if she's gonna be like that sometimes we don't see the point of being friends. We ask her to stop doing it and being bossy, but the next day she'll just start all over again but we're scared to tell her what we really feel to her face in case she won't wanna be our friend any more.' It was an upsetting session and even though the girls resolved to be kinder to one another, I didn't hold out much hope. They had embarked on the ritual sado-

masochistic dance typical of so many teenage girls, where one
friend gets picked upon but doesn't dare pull away to find new
friends or tell others.

Often everything seems to come to a head for girls at the age
of thirteen or fourteen and teachers when pressed will admit
that this age is usually a cesspit of teenage volatility. At fifteen
and sixteen girls have to focus on coursework and GCSEs and
they also tend to be more mature emotionally. But adolescent
turmoil seems to reach its peak at thirteen and the bitching
erupts like some vast boil. This is the year when large groups of
girls begin to character assassinate and splinter. Some experiment with adult pursuits – with drink, drugs and sex, and often
the groups split between those who do and those who don't.
Those who 'don't' may have greater willpower and a sense of
self-protection, but they are also often secretly envious of
aspects of the lives of girls who 'do'. They would like to know
what it's like, they fantasise and crave excitement. And
because these 'good' girls have also effectively absorbed the
message that good girls are nice, kind and nurturing, not mean,
they express their animosity and their disapproval verbally
rather than physically.

'Year 9 was such a nightmare because we had these really
tightly defined cliques and we just hated each other and it just
exploded,' says a girl who is now sixteen in Year 11. 'We were
just happy people in Years 7 and 8. There were three groups:
my group, which I'm proud to say were the nice group; and
then there was the sad group who kind of got pushed together
because nobody really liked them; and then there were the
complete bitches who came in every Monday and bragged
about how it was so fun over the weekend when they got

drunk or blah blah. They liked being the superior group on top of everything, but they actually hated each other. There were about ten to fifteen of them and they fought the whole time. The worst thing they did was isolate this one person, they just cut her off, ignored her and then when she got back into the group she joined with the others and turned on someone else. So she hadn't even learned from that experience not to do it.'

I spent months agonising over my own daughter when she was in Year 9. She spent most evenings in floods of tears on the phone, embroiled in such complicated scenarios over who had said or done what to whom that I couldn't begin to unravel what was going on and she didn't want to talk about it. I subsequently discovered, years later, when we were discussing bitching for this book, that she had been severely ostracised by girls she considered her closest friends. She had started a diary with one friend in which they both wrote down their most private thoughts and feelings. Her friend betrayed her by showing the book to others in the gang and from then on my daughter was out. They would start singing as she came into the classroom and for several weeks she was left out of social arrangements. As she told me this story, and I finally found out what had happened two years later, large tears rolled down her face. 'I've never felt so alone,' she said. 'It was like their code, she's coming, start singing.' The experience of being kicked out from the security of the gang still hurt even though most of these girls are still among her closest friends. It's a pain that can sear permanently. 'It's fantastic, the support that girls give each other and often these become permanent trusted friends,' says Adrienne Katz of Young Voice. 'But when you're excluded, dropped from the warmth of that embrace, it's a terrible thing; you lose that safety net and you lose your status.'

As girls grow older, become happier and more sure of themselves they grow out of such extreme levels of nastiness and bitch less. However, once the art of bitching is learned as a means of aggression and competition, women never lose that skill completely. They get better at it, camouflaging their hostility with far more subtle put-downs. These are described in full if you flip this book over to *The Big Fat Bitch Book For Grown-Up Girls*. When we feel vulnerable, insecure or threatened by another woman we resort to the same bitch tactics that we learned in the playground. So that can be at seventeen when you're under pressure and feeling competitive over exams, university entrance and boys; at twenty-seven in an overly competitive industry like banking or acting; or at thirty-seven as mothers made to feel inadequate by other mothers at the school gate. When good friends get together for a good bitch, it's great fun and can be hugely funny. But there's always this sense that there is something shameful about it. We all feel embarrassment the day after when we know we have gone too far. But that doesn't mean you're a bad person. With greater awareness of why we bitch, we recognise true spite for what it is and can really relish the enjoyment and wit of great bitching with true friends that much more.

~

On the window-ledge beside mine, Cordelia and Grace and Carol are sitting, jammed in together, whispering and giggling. I have to sit on a window-ledge by myself because they aren't speaking to me. It's something I said wrong, but I don't know what it is because they won't tell me. Cordelia says it will be better for me to think back over everything I've said today and try to pick out the wrong thing. That way I will learn not to say such a thing again. When I've guessed the right answer, then they will speak to me again. All of this is for my own good, because they are my best friends and they want to help me improve.

From *Cat's Eye* by Margaret Atwood

How Do I Hate Thee?
Let Me Count the Ways

- Gossiping just loud enough to be overheard; evil looks; blanking; whispering; eye-rolling
- Starting rumours. The best I heard was about a girl whose boyfriend said he would only go out with her if she would do the three Hs: give 'head', do his homework and get high with him. Truth or rumour? Either way it's bitchy
- Texting nasty messages or sending pictures with nasty messages attached to them
- Sending postcards. 'We're really (not) missing you'
- Secret bitch books, hate clubs, truth circles, petitions, 'Trash X websites'
- Pinning notes up around school. One girl who phoned Childline had 'go away and die' written all over her belongings
- Hair pulling, stepping on somebody's foot or bumping into them in the corridors accidentally on purpose and then saying 'sorry' in a way that is clearly not meant
- Saying something nasty disguised as a joke – 'I was just kidding, can't you take a joke?' The person is then labelled as hypersensitive

- Conference calls where one girls stays silent while the other encourages the third person to say nasty things about the silent one
- 'The best buzz you get is to look at someone, then look at someone else and start giggling. It makes them feel *this* small.' Marysha, fifteen
- Leaving messages on answerphones – 'Have you got your pregnancy test back yet?' knowing that the parents are likely to hear this first
- Not leaping to someone's defence when they put themselves down
- Snatching food at lunch – 'You don't want that do you? Aren't you my friend?'
- 'If you don't help me/do this, I'll tell X that you said she was 'fat/a slut/an ugly cow . . .'
- Publicly leaving someone out in games at primary school. The worst example Marjorie Harness Goodwin found for her book *The Hidden Life of Girls* was with an African–American working-class girl who was continually left out of games. With bidding as to who would go first in a game she said 'I'm first!' 'No,' replied another girl. 'You're not even here'
- Exchanging secrets seemingly as equals – the gullible one will divulge something that is true, the bitch will make something up and then spread the true secret around. The determined bitch bully will make sure she knows all sorts of personal details about the person she is targeting
- Encouraging bad dressing by saying something looks nice when it doesn't. I came across two incidents interviewing teenage girls. Both were revealed with pride as triumphs.

One group of fifteen-year-olds had picked on a friend who thought she had great dress sense. They encouraged her to wear 'really clashing clothes, this red crushed-velvet vintagey top with green jeans and then she goes to a party and everyone laughs about it.' Another group of fourteen-year-olds helped a friend who wanted to dye her hair blonde. They felt she was getting too vain and irritating. So they kept telling her it was going to look really good, but failed to tell her that the dye was orange rather than blonde. 'It seems mean now but at the time it was funny. She deserved it,' says Karen, 'she stole one of our friend's boyfriends at a party, she said how much she liked him and kissed him in front of her'

- Ranking people in their group. Someone has to come bottom. 'Who do you like more?' 'Let's go through the class and see who needs plastic surgery'
- Fishing for compliments . . .
  'Do you think we're very pretty/clever/interesting or just average?'
  'Well, you're very pretty/clever/interesting, I'm just pretty average'
  'No, no, I think we're both just average'
- Telling on someone to a teacher, usually about swearing, or deliberately getting another into trouble
- Making up a fake band and pretending to like them so that the person targeted says they like them too without knowing
- Arranging to meet someone for a party and then not showing up, or worse – encouraging someone to have a party and then nobody showing up

- 'When you hear aspects of a secret from someone about another person you go up to that person and drop hints that you know to get it out of her.' Hannah, fifteen

- Bitching via instant messaging seems to arouse the most anger. 'MSN is the worst because there's no tone. When you say something to someone you can use tone to lighten it and let someone know it's a joke. You can't show emotion whereas when you fight at school you can hug and cry,' says Jamilla. It's also there for you to read over and over again. It doesn't go away. 'I had this argument with a girl on MSN and she printed it off and took it to school to show everyone,' says Clare. 'When I found out I just laughed. It's so pathetic that she needs this evidence. She's not good with words so I suppose she wouldn't have been able to tell people what we said without it. I called her on the phone to try and sort it out but she just went silent on me'

- When I interviewed Rosalind Wiseman, the author of *Queen Bees and Wannabes*, I asked for the worst example she had come across recently in her work talking to girls in school. 'Two girls, one a boarder and the other lived up the road, and they were such good friends that they swapped passwords. Then they had a massive fight and the boarder got into the other girl's account and sent an email to lots of people saying there would be a party that weekend. All of these people showed up and she didn't know why and then the school found out and she was threatened with expulsion. The school didn't believe her when she said she hadn't done it, I wouldn't have believed her either, but the school took it seriously and investigated which computer

the emails had been sent from. That is evil! When girls do something this nasty it's because they think something wrong has been done to them and that justifies their behaviour. They think 'I'm gonna show her that she can't mess with me'

CADY: And they have this book, this burn book, where they write mean things about all the girls in our grade.

JANIS: What does it say about me?

CADY: (*lying because the book describes Janis as a dyke*) You're not in it.

JANIS: Those bitches!

Mean Girls

Two six-year-olds are two of the brightest girls in their class. X is the eldest with five brothers and sisters. Y is younger and an only child. Both girls put their name forward for election as form captain in the autumn term. X wins. She consequentially becomes more popular and Y spends the rest of the term trying to be her friend. At the beginning of the spring term there is a new election for form captain. X wants to win again, she cannot bear not to be the best and senses that Y is vulnerable as a younger, only child. So she rustles support, tells all her friends not to vote for Y. Children vote by raising their hands and closing their eyes. But Y cheats, opens her eyes and sees how many of the others have ganged up against her.

**Anecdote related by child psychoanalyst
Margot Waddell**

Insecurity Breeds Contempt
(and self contempt)

Put it this way: if a girl can get through adolescence she can get through anything. Parents accuse you of being all sorts of things – selfish, untidy, preoccupied with your friends and always on the phone, but they don't know half of what you live with as a teenager, do they? Late childhood to adolescence is the peak time for loss of confidence and self-esteem in a person's life. How you look really matters. You want clothes you can't afford. There's pressure at school and at home. You want to go out but there's nowhere much for you to go, and anyway you haven't got any money. You feel like lots of different people trapped inside one growing, changing body that often you don't much like. You crave independence, fame, fortune, your own home, love, sexual experience, fun, to be understood but it's all so scary out there. But you don't want to be made to feel like a child either. Most young women feel all of these things deeply, often all at the same time. Consequently, they have a sixth sense detecting these insecurities in others and manage to hit upon them with astonishing accuracy when they're feeling particularly vulnerable. 'We locate weaknesses in others that we cannot bear in ourselves,' says adolescent psychotherapist Jeannie Milligan. 'When you feel vulnerable you become autocratic and controlling of others. Adolescents are not in control of their own lives, so they like to give the false illusion that at least they can be in control of someone else.' When you bitch about someone else, you put yourself in a superior position – you have the correct moral values, the better fashion sense, they don't. By lashing out at others, teenagers deflect attention from their own failings. The best defence is offence. 'We like to think we're bitching because we're being played unfairly,' says Juliet, who is fourteen, 'but the real reason is that we feel threatened by people, that they might be trying to take something of ours.' Young people don't feel that they have much spare to lose. In this section of *The Big Fat Bitch Book*, young people and experts talk about all of the insecurities associated with growing up and the way those get targeted for bitching. These insecurities live on when we become adults and women continue to bitch about each other's looks, sex lives, status, marriages and friendships whenever they feel the need to bond or make themselves feel morally superior.

Appearance

When has Pink not been copying me? In her fashion and so on, it's always like, 'Gosh, I just wore that last week.'

Christina Aguilera

It's not who you are that matters, it's what you wear, who you hang out with and what they're wearing. Image, having the right label, being 'cool' is everything. 'In some cases if you haven't got all the names and all the tags or have your hair done in a certain way then you're not really in the group, which is wrong,' says Annette, who is fifteen. Girls in particular judge each other by what they are wearing and how they look because appearance is so important in the mating game.

Evolutionary psychologists believe that it all comes down to sex and the biological urge to reproduce the species and our own genetic brilliance. If we summarise it in the simplest terms it goes something like this – men have their entire lifespan to reproduce and can afford to be choosy; women have limited opportunities with one chance at conception each month from their teens until the menopause. Men tend to value attractiveness and youth most in women because these aspects signify fertility, so girls and women compete vigorously with each other over how they look. Men can father children any number of times, but women have to be careful who they select. Men need to look fit (healthy genes to pass on), have good prospects (to be able to provide for a child) and be kind and loving (more likely to stay around). As all of you know only too well, boys that fall into all three categories are pretty thin on the ground. So competition and the need to put each other's appearance down is intense. 'If a girl comes into school without her hair done all the other girls will say "Oh, she's a state,"' says Martin, 'but with the boys it doesn't matter.'

The most popular girls tend to be the ones who are best at imitating the images of womanhood they see in the media, which of course aren't representative of real womanhood at all. They pour over models and celebrities in fashion magazines, analysing their style and their cellulite and every innocent female passer-by gets the once-over. 'Girls bitch about your appearance whatever you wear, even if you're pretty but mainly if you're ugly,' says Emily, who is fourteen. 'Even though we go to a school with uniform we'll still be saying "Look at what she's wearing!" when she's wearing the same as us. Someone'll say, "Omigod! That skirt is soooo short" even if their own skirt is only like an inch longer. We all have to wear black shoes but if one person has a little star on it or something or gets a great pair of shoes then everyone wants the same but then you're accused of being a copycat and everybody bitches about that.'

'You go for a sleepover and everyone will be like so competitive about what you're wearing,' says Karen, who is fourteen. 'If I looked nice, the others want to compete, buy the same belt. Everyone wants to be the coolest, the best in our group.'

Girls play around with different images of womanhood and often make dreadful mistakes, dyeing their hair platinum blonde when they're a brunette or staggering along to a party in eight-inch high heels. They want to look more grown-up and they want to look sexy, but then they also don't want to look tarty, like an easy hit. It is hard to get the balance right, and often they don't. 'I dyed my hair blonde and I know it looks ridiculous and I'm going to dye it again this weekend,' says Georgia, who is fifteen. 'But I can tell people are talking about it and giving me dirty looks. It's unkind when someone makes a mistake and everyone talks about it. They don't let you forget it, ever. Its easy to do it to someone else but very difficult when it happens to you.'

When boys bitch about a girl it is usually over how she looks, for they are judging them too, piling on yet more insecurity. Girls need constant flattery and affirmation from each other. They fish for compliments with 'I'm so fat! My nose is massive! I hate my hair', knowing that someone in their tight-knit gang will leap to deny it and bolster that fragile image for just a few minutes. When someone tells a girl that she's fat (when she isn't), too thin or has too wide a forehead, she will find it hard not to believe them. 'If you have a fat boy and a fat girl, the girl will get called more things than the boy,' says Ben. 'With a boy you'd just have a laugh in a jokey way but with a girl it just makes them more depressed.' Being fat is the number-one insult on the teenage bitch hit list about appearance.

They also say things like:

'Look at your lunch!' (scathingly)
'Are *you* going to eat *that*?'
Or, they just cough, look at you oddly and then at your
   lunch.
Or, they pass a girl diet magazines under the desk in class.

One twelve-year-old girl who rang Childline had been targeted for so long that she said, 'I cry all the time. I'm living in
hell. Sometimes I don't eat or I skip meals because if I lose
weight it might stop.'

You can also be bitched about for being too thin ('she is definitely anorexic'). Headlice and body odour provoke countless
opportunities for comment. 'There are a lot of people who
smell in our class, so we call them "Salt and Vinegar",' say Sam
and Claudia. 'There's a girl from Bangladesh who eats a lot of
curry so we call her "Tikka Masala" and Caz is a good friend
but she has, shall we say, a bit of a problem (vaginal odour) so
we call her "fish and chips".' The problem is that girls tend to
want to be perfect. 'Everybody would like to be perfect, nice
figure, big boobs, pretty nice hair,' says Christine from Leeds,
'but the trouble is life just isn't like that, is it?'

SUSAN: Hey, Edie!
EDIE: Wow, get a load of you! You look so pretty I hardly
   recognise you.'

From *Desperate Housewives*

Pride and Prejudice
by Jane Austen

. . . while Mr Darcy was attending them to their carriage, Miss Bingley was venting her feelings in criticisms of Elizabeth's person, behaviour and dress. But Georgiana would not join her. Her brother's recommendation was enough to ensure her favour; his judgement could not err, and he had spoken in such terms of Elizabeth, as to leave Georgiana without the power of finding her otherwise than lovely and amiable. When Darcy returned to the saloon, Miss Bingley could not help repeating to him some part of what she had been saying to his sister.

'How very ill Eliza Bennet looks this morning, Mr Darcy,' she cried; 'I never in my life saw any one so much altered as she is since the winter. She is grown so brown and coarse! Louisa and I were agreeing that we should not have known her again.'

However little Mr Darcy might have liked such an address, he contented himself with coolly replying, that he perceived no other alteration than her being rather tanned, – no miraculous consequence of travelling in the summer.

'For my own part,' she rejoined, 'I must confess that I never could see any beauty in her. Her face is too thin; her complexion has no brilliancy; and her features are not at all handsome. Her nose wants character; there is nothing marked in its lines. Her teeth are tolerable, but not out of the common way; and as for her eyes, which have sometimes been called so fine, I never could perceive anything extraordinary in them. They have a sharp, shrewish look, which I do not like at all; and in her air altogether there is a self-sufficiency without fashion, which is intolerable.'

Persuaded as Miss Bingley was that Darcy admired Elizabeth, this was not the best method of recommending herself; but angry people are not always wise; and in seeing him at last look somewhat nettled, she had all the success she expected. He was resolutely silent however; and, from a determination of making him speak, she continued,

'I remember when we first knew her in Hertfordshire, how amazed we all were to find she was a reputed beauty; and I particularly recollect your saying one night, after they had been dining at Netherfield, "*She* a beauty! – I should as soon call her mother a wit." But afterwards she seemed to improve on you, and I believe you thought her rather pretty at one time.'

'Yes,' replied Darcy, who could contain himself no longer, 'but *that* was only when I first knew her, for it is many months since I have considered her as one of the handsomest women of my acquaintance.'

He then went away, and Miss Bingley was left to all the satisfaction of having forced him to say what gave no one any pain but herself.

Sexuality

I've got much more style than Jordan. I just don't go
out in a bra and knickers and I don't think I dress like
a tart.

Jodie Marsh

What you've got to remember is that Jodie Marsh is
trying to be like me anyway . . . she's trying to dress
like me, tone down her make-up like me and it's just
sad . . . If Jodie's into her sex like she says she is,
Scott's definitely not the one. Don't get me wrong,
he's a really nice guy, but he's rubbish in bed.

Jordan

~

Sex and sexuality are common topics for bitchathons. It's all so
exciting but confusing. How do you learn about how to do it,
and be sexy when a chaste, 'good' sexual reputation is also still
so important? Boys like loyalty and fidelity in a girl (how else
are they to know that any offspring is theirs?), so insulting each
other as 'slags' or 'ho's' and 'whores' is common. But then they
also want you to be sexual because they want someone to do it
with and insult girls as 'frigid' or 'lesbian' if they don't. Girls

need to preserve their own reputation by distancing themselves from the 'easy' ones. The number-one provocation for physical fights between young females is an attack on a girl's personal and sexual reputation.

Boys insult each other with 'You're so gay,' because most are frightened of being labelled homosexual themselves. 'The biggest insult in an all-girls' school is to be called a lesbian,' says Claudia, 'because then everyone feels uncomfortable around her. If anyone sits on her lap everyone goes whoa . . .!' Lily is fifteen and came out as a lesbian at her single-sex school at the age of thirteen, at great cost. She has few friends and is regularly ostracised. 'I don't see why I should avoid talking about it when all the others can talk openly about how they fancy boys. They bait me, call me a 'weirdo' or a 'freak' and pretend to be scared that I'll jump them or they say, Who do you fancy? and then tell her. I know I'm talked about a lot and that they think I'm odd and that really hurts.'

Rising sexual interest is never an issue for boys, but is often difficult for girls. Sexual experience still gives a boy status, while girls are easily typecast as 'slags', 'sluts', 'whores', or 'dogs'. Rumours are circulated in most schools that someone is pregnant when more often than not she isn't. 'If a lad and a girl are together,' says Martin from Wrexham, 'and the girl goes off with another lad, she's a slag, but if the lad does it – good job, mate.' And it's the girls who reinforce this unequal code. 'Some girls are really slutty, they go too far,' says Karen. 'Girls envy them but they also think "I can't believe she's done that".' In one school I visited, a fifteen-year-old girl was rumoured to be pregnant and had bravely stood up for herself one lunchtime by saying, 'Some people have been saying things about me that aren't very nice.' 'Yeah' came the reply from someone she considered a close friend, 'Well, it's your own friends who've been saying those things.'

At Juliet's school in Hastings, one girl they knew had met someone on the Internet and was planning to go on holiday with him. 'She's just a dog and her mother doesn't teach her right from wrong, she goes with lots of different guys and is really rude. She told me in secret about this holiday and told me not to tell anyone. She knows it's going to be seen as this really bad thing, so I told her that she shouldn't go. I can speak to her how I like because I know she really wants our approval, and then in media studies I turned round and told this other group of girls about what she was planning and then watched them put her down.'

'The nastiest thing is being called a "slag",' says Christine from Manchester. Teenagers throw words like 'slut' and 'flirt' at each other with wild abandon, but the definitions are often amorphous. When an adult uses the word 'flirt', it distinctly means giving someone a sexual come-on, but as a teenager, you don't really know how to flirt yet, you're experimenting with all things sexual, so 'flirt' can mean anything – just looking or talking to a boy, exchanging text messages or mucking about like kids in the playground – can lead to accusations or fights. 'Slut' in adult terms means someone who sleeps around. For a teenage girl just the fact that boys like her or even the slightest revelation of flesh is enough to be typecast.

You just have to do something once, like pull up your skirt or just wipe the hair out of your eyes and you'll gain a reputation and someone will say, 'Omigod you're such a slut.'

Janine, fifteen

~

You don't have to actually get boys to be a slut. Just grabbing their arm and dancing with them is enough. Girls get popular by being with boys. You're hated because of it but followed because when you go to a party the boys will follow you.

Anna, fourteen

~

Most girls communicate with boys by flirting, and girls do crave attention especially from boys. If you flirt with someone you know that someone else likes, that's a big issue for girls and people do that a lot without thinking about it. If someone's going out with a boy and another girl cheats with him, then the bitching goes on for ages and the whole class takes sides.

Bella, fifteen

~

You just do one little thing and they don't let you
forget about it. It's something really small like I used
to fancy this boy and still people are saying 'Yeah,
you wanna marry him, you wanna meet your in-
laws.'

Mariella, fifteen

~

This new boy starts and I sit next to him so I helped
him with something he didn't understand, that's all,
I was just helping the poor guy because he was new
and the next thing I know Philip spreads it round that
I fancy him.

Alysha, fifteen

Teenage boys of the same age tend to be shorter and less
mature (their growth spurt occurs at the end of the pubertal
process) and there just aren't enough good-looking ones to go
round. Consequently, the fighting between girls can be particularly vicious, gathering together to discuss the boys and
exchange confidences about which ones they fancy, and then
the squabbling begins, often in unseemly ways. When Lucy
started sixth form at a larger co-educational school she soon
found someone she fancied. When she told a new friend who
had been at the school since the age of eleven that she liked
him, that friend told her to go for it, so she did at a party the
following Saturday night. A huge row erupted and Lucy found
herself being screamed at by the very same tearful girl who had

omitted to tell her that she was in love with him. Lucy left the party in floods of tears while the boy in question just shrugged and went off for another dance. The following Monday at school Lucy's friend apologised grudgingly. She then sat on a wall with her old friends around her and said self-importantly – 'I just find that this year we all seem to have got bitchier. I don't know whether it's the clothes and not having to wear uniform or what.' She stared straight at Lucy, who knew exactly what she meant. The new intake of girls had threatened the status quo of existing cliques and alliances.

~

As You Like It by William Shakespeare
Rosalind to Phoebe, Act 3 Scene 5

And why, I pray you?
Who might be your mother
That you insult, exult, and all at once,
Over the wretched? What though you have no beauty –
As, by my faith, I see no more in you
Than without candle may go dark to bed –
Must you therefore be proud and pitiless?
Why, what means this? Why do you look on me?
I see no more in you than in the ordinary
Of Nature's sale-work. – 'Od's my little life,
I think she means to tangle my eyes, too!
No, faith, proud mistress, hope not after it.
'Tis not your inky brows, your black silk hair,
Your bugle eyeballs, nor your cheek of cream,

That can entame my spirits to your worship.
(*to Silvius*) You, foolish shepherd, wherefore do you
    follow her,
Like foggy south, puffing with wind and rain?
You are a thousand times a properer man
Than she a woman. 'Tis such fools as you
That makes the world full of ill-favour'd children.
'Tis not her glass, but you, that flatters her,
And out of you she sees herself more proper
Than any of her lineaments can show her.
(*to Phoebe*) But, mistress, know yourself; down on your
    knees
And thank heaven, fasting, for a good man's love;
For I must tell you friendly in your ear,
Sell when you can; You are not for all markets.

Identity

Teenagers create their own rules for belonging to a larger group because it's much too scary being out there as a distinct individual. They play around with images and ideas and depend heavily on their friends to help them determine a sense of their own uniqueness, a sense of self. In her memoir about being fat, *Eating Myself*, Candida Crewe recalls how she was playing a truth game at school in 1976 when she was twelve. They were sitting in a circle going round telling each girl what they thought were her good and bad characteristics. 'When it came to my turn there was a long pause, silence as everyone scratched their heads for inspiration as to my positive points. They were about to give up but eventually someone piped up, 'I know! Candida has very good diction.'

A girl's sense of self is inextricably linked with how women are seen and portrayed in the wider world and they look keenly at culture, their mothers and other women for definition. We can't help but judge ourselves by judging others and it's a habit that few of us lose. 'We need a sense of ourselves within an invisible hierarchical pecking order,' says novelist Elizabeth Noble. 'You could take any woman aside at a party and she would be able to tell you who was the thinnest or the fattest there, who was married and who wasn't, who was frumpily dressed, even what handbags they were carrying. It's like this scanning system that we have.' And then we like to talk about all this with each other.

Gossip plays a key part in all of our lives and helps define who we are and the type of lives we want to lead. Women are particularly good at talking intimately, getting at the nitty-gritty of emotions and what motivates us. Gossip is essentially good for us. When we express approval of each other, when we reassure and flatter we help to reduce uncertainties and shore up each other's sense of self. We trigger endorphins in much the same way as physical touch. The psychologist Robin Dunbar believes that gossip is the human equivalent of the grooming that takes place amongst primates and evolved because physical grooming takes up too much time amongst larger social networks. When we talk about other people we share and reinforce a common code of behaviour. Gossip signifies group membership. To be part of a group you must be able to understand and participate in the gossip of that group, whatever your age, at school, the golf club or the school gate. Gossip circulates essential information about individual cultures, it strengthens relationships and we now have many more ways to cement those bonds with mobiles, email and instant messaging.

But the information transmitted through gossip can also be used as a powerful weapon against us. Teenagers trust each other with deep secrets, inhibitions and uncertainties about who they are, only to find that knowledge circulated by people they thought were friends. With the mind changes of adolescence we all become much more aware of our own unique weirdness, that terrifying sense of existential aloneness as we grapple with the fact that it's down to our efforts alone to make something of our lives. So teenagers bitch about anyone who is not just like them to deflect attention from their own weirdnesses. Everybody else is either a 'freak,' 'weirdo, 'chav' (common), 'boffin' (nerd) or 'beck' (Jewish girl). 'My friends tease me, they say "Look at you, Little Beck", just because I live in Mill Hill,' complained a girl in one of the bitching discussions I chaired in a school in London.

'That's because you share something that gentiles don't,' replied a non-Jewish girl in the year above her.

'But that doesn't mean I should be locked out of social activities with the girls who aren't Jewish.'

Race becomes crucial for a teenager's sense of self, but is also a target for taunts and bullying. 'I used to go to a different school,' says Leila who is half-Turkish and lives in the northwest. 'But then all the racist comments got really bad when I was thirteen. This girl used to just push me all the time and then there were these notes being passed around calling me a "smelly cow" and "paki". I did try and earn my respect back, this girl flicked me with an elastic band so I punched her in the face. Then I changed schools and that really helped but I still get the odd comment. You learn how to take it.'

As each girl struggles to grow up and discover her individuality, she finds herself coming into conflict with the group of friends she has been defined by. 'If you're different then you're going to get bitched about.' Bella is fourteen. 'But then if you're too much the same as everyone else you're gonna get bitched about too because if someone started copying me I'd say "Oh, they're such a loser", so you can't win. People don't want you to be who you are and you're afraid to stand out or be who you are. Someone actually told me that they didn't like me just because I was me.'

Bitching sessions often start when a girl makes a dangerous request of a friend in an attempt to know herself better, 'Tell me what you don't like about me.' When girl number two doesn't hold back because teenagers tend to lack the more adult skills of tact and diplomacy, girl number one gets upset and hits back with 'Well, I don't like it when you . . .' Once Pandora's Box is open, all that pent-up frustration that comes from not saying what you really think about someone who has been irritating you for weeks erupts with accusations of being two-faced, hypocritical, vain or selfish.

Being bitchy distinguishes a girl. She's a cut above, popular, powerful, no one dares mess with her.

When you bitch, you're seen as powerful because you're controlling people, you don't get bullied back.

Leila, fifteen

~

You're spreading something and everyone will then come to you and say 'Did you really say that? That's so mean!'

Emily, fourteen

~

Being part of the popular group means you have to have a persona, it's a prerequisite to be bitchy.

Lily, fifteen

~

Girls need to act hard in front of their mates, then they know who you are, they don't think you're somebody else.

Karen, thirteen

~

I've got power over two people in our year, haven't I? Ian and Steven. It's funny though, if I say to Steven 'Shut up' he says 'OK OK,' or 'I'll give you a quid to leave me alone' and I just say 'Shut up, Steven.'

Kirsty, fifteen

Most girls want to be popular even if that means not being liked because of the power they exude. They get bitched about but usually they don't care, the attention makes them feel like somebodies. Annie is fourteen and not in a popular gang. 'The nice part about being popular is that everyone knows who you are. It's hard to imagine someone bitching about me. I can't imagine what they'd say and that opens up a whole other can of worms about me.'

~

Dear Diary,

Heather told me she teaches people real life, she said real life sucks losers dry. You wanna fuck with the eagles, you have to learn to fly . . .

HEATHER 1: If you're gonna openly be a bitch . . .

VERONICA: Heather, why can't we talk to different types of people?

HEATHER: Fuck me gently with a chainsaw! Do I look like Mother Teresa? If I did I probably wouldn't mind talking to the geek squad. (*She looks over at the geek table in the canteen*)

GEEK: (*splutters his drink*) 'Did you see that? Heather Number One just looked right at me!

VERONICA: Doesn't it worry you that everyone in this school thinks you're a piranha?

HEATHER: Like I give a shit. They all want me as a friend or a fuck. I'm worshipped at Westerburg and I'm only a junior.

From *Heathers* (1989), in which all three girls in the most popular set are called Heather

'Good Girls Are Just Bad Girls Who Don't Get Caught'

Kelly, fifteen

I'll come and make love to you at five o'clock. If I'm late start without me.

Tallulah Bankhead

When sexual reputation means so much more to a girl than it does to a boy, preserving the 'Good Girl' façade is crucial. And that's where the skill of duplicity takes hold. Girls soon learn how to pretend to be what's expected of them, suppressing anything that appears to be too overtly unfeminine. 'Good' girls are thin and keep their mouths shut, mask their emotions, are self-effacing and nice to everyone and they don't swear or sleep around. But any girl with more than an ounce of intelligence can see that she needs a great many other skills which appear to contradict the 'good' girl image if she also wants to succeed. The real girl loves food, feels sexy, has opinions and ambitions. She needs to compete, strive, show her strengths, be outspoken and persistent. We're surrounded by explicit sexual imagery of women on advertising hoardings, magazines and television yet when teenage girls try to imitate them they're labelled as 'sluts'. 'With stuff like *The* OC the girls are always showing their legs and wearing tons of make-up and it's almost like saying this is what you're supposed to do when you're older,' says Emily, who is fourteen. And these contradictions are confusing when you're a teenager tussling with what sort of a woman you would like to be. 'The same old gender dichotomies hold sway: girls will be girly-girls or they will be tomboys; they will be good girls or sluts, nice girls or bitches,' says Lyn Mikel Brown, in her book *Girlfighting*. 'While the parameters have shifted a bit, the general structure hasn't changed – both sides provide pathways to power through boys' attention and acceptance.'

Girls are now brought up to believe in their ability to do anything they want and the expectation is that they will earn their own living. Yet the inequities between boyworld and girlworld grow clearer as young women become more aware of the wider world outside their childhood. I visited dozens of different schools around the country interviewing teenage girls for this book. At one session with a group of girls who attended 'girls group' with a youth worker because they had been getting into trouble, the anger was palpable but they were unable to articulate why. When I opened up the discussion and asked them what sort of pressures girls live with in the wider world, I couldn't shut them up. They had something else to bitch about and blame for their own troubles:

You have to look nice, you've got loads of pressure going to school and you've gotta watch what you do and where you go all the time.

Lorna, fifteen

~

Boys can defend themselves, they're stronger they don't have to watch themselves and get scared of getting raped or having unwanted kids. It's all right for the lads 'cos they can get a lady pregnant and then just walk off. Boys may get raped but I can't remember the last time I watched the news and heard about a boy being raped.

Jackie, fourteen

~

Periods, why do girls get 'em and the lads don't? I wish they did.

Alysha, fifteen

In her book *Girlfighting*, Lyn Mikel Brown argues convincingly that it is because the power girls have tends to come from qualities they have little control over, 'their looks, their vulnerability, their accommodation to others' wants and needs, their feminine wiles,' that they take out their frustration and anger on each other. 'Girls and women derogate and judge and reject other girls and women for the same reasons they fear being derogated and judged and rejected – for not matching up to feminine ideals of beauty and behaviour or for being brave enough not to care. Girls meanness to other girls is a result of their struggle to make sense of or to reject their secondary status in the world and to find ways to have power and to experience feeling powerful.'

Teenage girls know how hard it is to maintain the 'Good

Girl' ideal. They become chameleons, changing according to who they're with, merging in with what others want them to be and soon learn how to manipulate the situation for their own benefit. Signs of 'perfection' in others raise anxieties. Anyone who excels or exhibits too much success is threaten-ing. She is liable to get bitched about as either 'attention seeking' or 'too up herself' to be brought back into line. 'There are certain groups where everyone turns against one person who was really popular because they've had enough of her. They think she's too vain or selfish, two-faced or up herself,' says Hannah. 'Then we try and bring her down, not compli-ment her. We do it for her own good because she's starting to get unattractive. It's also about learning how to be tough enough to take it.' Girls say they are seeking to protect their friends from damaging themselves with 'sluttish, bad girl' behaviour because they care about them, but often they just feel so profoundly insecure about who they are that they police each other vigilantly to make sure nobody steps out of line and makes them feel small.

When a girl transgresses the social code and strays into bad girl territory she risks the reputation of the entire group. Claudia and Sam told me about a major falling out with one of their close friends after a scene at a bonfire night party when some 'rude boys' gatecrashed. Their friend allowed one of them to jump on her and lick her face. Claudia went round calling her a 'ho' (whore) at school after the party. 'I got really angry with her and now I don't invite her out with us because I know what she's capable of. The next day she sent me this text saying "I hate you! You've ruined my life . . . and what's Hannah's number" – the fact that she could say that! Trying to take my friend away from me! . . . I rang her that night but she refused to pick up. We did eventually sort it out and it is better now but no one really trusts her. If she keeps doing that with random people she'll get into trouble. I want to protect her, she's younger than us so I feel that we have to. When we go to parties she wants to wear short miniskirts and heels while we want to wear jeans so *she* calls *us* "frigid bitches".'

Girls maintain their reputation as 'good' by hanging the 'bad' label onto somebody else, identifying someone else's vices as worse than their own. At one of the schools I visited in Manchester a group of fifteen-year-old girls had turned on one of their friends when she took her clothes off in front of a group of boys at a party. 'It's disgusting, it's wrong what she did,' says Kirsty, the most articulate and confident of the gang of ten. I subsequently discovered that this Queen Bitch had been forced to move 200 miles with her mother to get away from an alcoholic, abusive father. Martha's offence had taken place six months earlier but she had never been told what she had done to offend them, just ostracised. 'People turned against me,' says Martha in front of Kirsty, 'and I never knew why, until now.' Emotions rose as they began to confront the issue and I asked them why this prank was so bad, so offensive, when they would have laughed at a boy who had done the same thing. Why did it warrant such an extreme and prolonged punishment? One girl began to cry and ran out of the room and Kirsty got defensive. 'Everyone bitches about each other,' she shouted angrily, for hurtful bitching is veiled aggression and she clearly had a great deal of vulnerability to protect. 'I've bitched about *you* [pointing to a girl] and *you* [pointing to another girl] and not so much about you and you because I don't know so much about you to bitch about,' and then she denied that she had turned on Martha in the first place.

Denouncing others gains recognition, approval from adults as well as power within the group, and quickly becomes a habit when girls do not understand the reasons or the implications of what they are doing. By the time they reach adulthood they continue to highlight the weaknesses and vices of others as a way of maintaining their own position at work or in any situation where they feel insecure. As adults we all have a tendency to expect more of women than we do of men. We assume they will be good; kinder, more selfless, more honest and trustworthy, and we dislike overt sexual come-ons in women and see them as 'tarts' – while men are full of charm as womanisers. The idea that a mother could abuse or abandon her own child is so abhorrent and foreign to the notion of the 'good' mother that we all aspire to be, that feelings of hate or aggression towards our own children seem shameful and evidence of failure rather than natural consequences of a stressful role. But there are no 'good' girls or 'bad' girls; just real girls struggling with a vast array of contradictory cultural messages and expectations as well as trying to have a good time.

~

(*Sleepover at Frenchy's house. Frenchy offers Sandy a cigarette*)
SANDY: No thanks, I don't smoke.
FRENCHY: You don't? Go ahead, try it, it won't kill yer.
(*Sandy inhales and coughs*)
RIZZO: Oh I forgot to tell you, you shouldn't inhale unless
you're used to it.
(*others laugh*)

(*The other girls put on wigs imitating Sandy and sing 'Look at Me I'm Sandra Dee/Lousy with virginity/Won't go to bed till I'm legally wed/I can't, I'm Sandra Dee.'*)

SANDRA: Are you making fun of me, Riz?
RIZZO: (*pulls off wig*) Some people are so touchy.

From *Grease* (1978)

Friendship

Girls' friendships are as intense and passionate as love affairs, touching and hugging each other, flirting and whispering in each other's ears and falling out like lovers too, deeply jealous when they suspect that 'best' friends have been unfaithful. Girls want to be with each other almost all the time. When close girlfriends are together, and away from boys, they often have the best fun. They are liberated from feminine stereotypes and allowed to be themselves. Girls in gatherings or at sleepovers become that much louder, more raucous and more argumentative than they might dare to be otherwise and they bitch to bond. 'Sleepovers are just an excuse to bitch,' says Ros. 'People pretend to bitch about someone just to be in the conversation and in the group. They even bitch about people they like. You can't not bitch. You should walk away when someone's bitching and not get involved but then they might think you're being the bitch for walking away and talk about you.'

Girls' friendship groups are so intense that it is often hard to be completely honest with one another. You spend so much time in each other's company, and then hours on the phone dissecting the significance of who said or did what to whom that it is easy to get irritated by one another. But you can't say so in case you hurt their feelings. 'When you're in a bad mood or having a bad day you bitch about one of your mates,' says Alisha, 'but if you said it to their faces there'd probably be no gang at all because you'd row so much about it you'd break up. I could be closer to Amy than to anyone else in the group this week, but next week it could be totally different.' And then there's the difficulty of dealing with someone you no longer like or trust as a friend when you don't know how to disassociate yourself from her. As adults with more space between you, you can just let a friendship slide, but that's much harder when you're young or with that person all of the time at school. 'I'm currently friends with this girl who I don't particularly like and it's really difficult to tell her because nobody really likes to be told that somebody doesn't like them,' says Anita who is twelve and has just started at a new secondary school and formed a quick friendship with someone she thought she liked. 'I wouldn't like to be told that so I'm trying to cope with it but it is really hard.' If you wait for them to do something to you, you're then allowed to push them away without feeling guilt. 'If you don't like someone you wait for them to do something to you,' says Kirsty from Manchester. 'You wait for them to step out of line so that you can go for 'em.'

'It's hard when you have a group of friends who dislike one because everyone refuses to acknowledge that they dislike this person but as soon as she's gone out the room it all comes out and they have this massive bitch about her,' says Claudia who is fifteen at an all-girls' school in London. 'It's really difficult not to be two-faced,' agrees Karen who goes to the same school. 'If you were bitching about someone behind her back and then she comes into the room you'd be really nice to her, it just comes naturally.' And because every girl knows this, there also lurks an uncomfortable anxiety – if we talk like this about others, what do they say about me when I'm not here?

> **You can never say something to someone and then say 'Don't tell anyone' because they will, they have to. They go up to someone else they want to be close to and say 'I promised I wouldn't tell anyone but . . .' It makes even the silliest thing seem more exciting.**
>
> Marisha, fifteen

~

> **If Sam tells me something private and tells me not to tell anyone but someone sees us talking, she'll come up to me and ask me what she said. If I then say I'm not allowed to say, she'll go 'You're so mean' and then blank me for the rest of the day.**
>
> Claudia, fifteen

All women gain huge amounts of guidance and support from their female friends. Establishing intimate friendships with other women helps us get through all the shit life throws at us, it keeps us healthy, and who knows, one day they may even find that female friendships are one of the main reasons why women live longer than men, who don't tend to have such intense support structures other than with their girlfriend. The comfort and support teenage girls get from each other is so important that exclusion or isolation is their worst fear. We make such an investment in our female friendships that we expect greater loyalty and commitment in return and will do anything to ensure against rejection, enduring incredible levels of hostility and humiliation rather than risk losing a 'friend'. Tight-knit friendship groups of girls typically rotate their nastiness. One girl becomes the focus of teasing and gets left out of plans. The others gain a sense of exhilarating power, that great rush that comes from feeling included when someone else is being left out and their bond of friendship feels unbreakable. 'In those moments', writes Rachel Simmons in *Odd Girl Out*, 'friendship feels pure, unthreatened and free of insecurity.' Most girls will themselves have felt the pain of isolation, of being excluded at some point in the past. Ganging up against others insures against feeling that isolation again.

When girls are at the receiving end they go to great lengths to hide their feelings. They pretend they don't mind and are not sad about being left out of social arrangements or dressed down for the way they look in the canteen. They go along with it, laugh it off, pretend to agree with group views even when they don't. 'It's easier to not care than to try and make accusations I can't prove,' says Lily, who is regularly ostracised and accused of making things up. 'Some people can be really horrible but you still wanna be with them,' says Jamilla, who is fourteen. 'You have to be careful not to show them that you've been hurt by something as they pick up on it and use it against you.'

When teenage girls speak out against group pressure they tend to get labelled as bossy and arrogant ('bad girl') in presuming to hold the higher moral ground. The accusation gets downplayed with 'Joke – can't you take a joke?' or chucked back in their face with 'Well, you shouldn't have been listening.' Or the victim gets something they did wrong dredged up from the past so that it's left as all their own fault. When Lily tries to talk to one friend 'about how she treats me, she gets annoyed and says "We're not having that conversation are we?" and walks away or signs off.' It's a surreal world with no reason. 'Once this girl was being really mean to me so I said something like "Piss off" and then *she* turned round to *me* and said "Stop being such a bitch!"' Jamilla recounts. The bully controls others by maintaining that only her version of events is true. There is no room for debate.

Often it is the really kind and good girl, the one people turn to for sensible, motherly advice who gets picked on by the girl in the group with the greatest 'sins' and insecurity. The 'good' girl is an easy target and she is also the one who is most likely to see their true weaknesses and betray them to others. 'It's not just girls trying to impress boys, it's girls trying to impress girls and they'll do anything to get them to like them, like pack their bag or do their homework,' says Clare, 'and then everyone'll end up bitching about them for being too nice. People use them and then it's the people who use who end up bitching about them the most.'

The danger is that arguments can escalate easily. 'Sometimes when you stand back and ask yourself what the argument's about, you don't even know,' says Rebecca. 'Most of the time it's not meant to hurt, it's a bit of sport, copying what they see in adverts or on the TV,' says Hazel Norbury, who has been a counsellor at Childline for thirteen years. 'But then it's like the mob thing, it spirals out of control and you're glad someone else is the victim because it lets you off the hook.'

REGINA: We do not have a clique problem at this school.

GRETCHEN: But you do have to look out for 'Frenemies'.

REGINA: What are 'Frenemies'?

GRETCHEN: Frenemies are enemies who act like friends. We call them 'Frenemies'.

KAREN: Or 'Enemends'.

GRETCHEN: Or friends who secretly hate you, we call the 'Fraitors'.

REGINA: (*rolls eyes*) That is so gay.

KAREN: (*gasps*) What if we called them 'Mean-em-aitors'?

REGINA: (*scoffs*)

GRETCHEN: No, honey, it has to have the word 'friend' in it.

KAREN: Oh . . .

Mean Girls

Emotions

It is all about anger. When you're unhappy you don't give a shit about what anybody else feels. If you're not happy with yourself and you're angry because someone's pissed you off, you take it out on someone who doesn't need it to be taken out on, which is wrong but it's right in a way. You need to do something to get it all out otherwise you just break down, everything inside you.

Marisha, fifteen

There's a lot to be emotional about and don't believe your parents when they patronise you by saying it's just your hormones. There's far more to it than that – how you look, who you are, friendships, the future, families. Teenagers get angry often, play loud music, kick the walls, shout at their parents and pick fights with their siblings. Girls get angry about the expectations they now have to meet as young women – about feeling sexual and not being able to express it, about having to be feminine when they don't want to be and by the way their friendships become so volatile. But they're not supposed to show it. Jealousy, anger, competitiveness and sexual desire have to be swallowed and suppressed in order to conform to feminine ideals. You can't get angry with boys if you also crave their approval. You can't rage at society because that might ruin your place in it. You can't even tell those closest to you exactly how you feel because such honesty could be hurtful, so instead teenage girls 'employ small armies of mediators,' writes Rachel Simmons, to do their work for them, 'usually willing friends who are uncomfortably caught in the middle or eager for the moments of intimacy that result from lending a hand to someone in trouble.'

When girls get stressed they have to let out all that pent up frustration and rage somewhere, so they pick at their own bodies, tear labels off bottles, bite their nails or rip pieces of paper into tiny pieces. 'School is like a pressure cooker, you get picked on by teachers, blamed for things you didn't do, get branded as the naughty bad girls and you just argue all the time so I just stand there when I'm frustrated and pull my hair until it hurts and then I feel better,' says Marisha. Her friend nods with recognition, 'I scratch my face.' And they love to stir things up a bit by bitching about each other behind their backs. 'It's healthy to bitch, you can't help it because if you don't tell anyone what you think about other people it gets bottled up and then you just go "I HATE YOU" one day and then every-one will hate you and the whole world will interfere,' says Emily, who is twelve. 'There are times when you just wanna hit someone, but you can't,' says Rebecca. 'All this stuff's been building up for ages and it all just comes out, you say all these things before you've even realised what you've said and you feel better afterwards.' 'I like making people feel bad; it makes me feel better,' says Harriet. 'You want someone else to feel as upset as you, you wanna show people how you feel,' says Olivia.

Little girls and boys express their anger in exactly the same ways. They throw tantrums, they push, hit or snatch toys. Once they go to school they watch and copy older children and adults inculcate age-old notions of masculinity and femininity without even noticing it. Girls are supposed to be kind; boys just fight. Physical aggression is discouraged more often in girls than in boys by parents and teachers. One study conducted by the University of Michigan in 1999 found that girls were told to be quiet, or to use a 'nicer' voice about three times more often than the boys, even though the boys were louder. By the time children reach the age of eight or nine, girls and boys are quite clear about the differences between them. Boys don't cry; girls do. Boys kick balls and fight; girls don't. Adults consider girls to be more mature than boys but actually they are just more adept at masking their true feelings. Bitching is always veiled anger. When someone says something horrible about you or someone else, consider the emotions behind the words. Why might they feel this way? In extreme cases, suppressed anger can lead to sadness and depression, eating disorders and self-harm. Grace Bowman, author of A Shape of My Own, became severely anorexic when she got into Cambridge after a childhood filled with triumph. 'I was the eldest, super-achieving, everything was perfect and I felt that I shouldn't show my emotions,' she told me. Her twin sisters are six years younger and not anorexic. 'They're completely different characters, they express themselves and they don't want to please everyone all of the time.'

It can be hard for 'good' girls to accept that they can feel a deep violent hatred for somebody or that they have a streak of cruelty in them, just like the boys. Teenagers need to feel the extremes of all those emotions, they crave excitement, scare themselves stupid with horror films and experiment with danger in order to feel and to understand the limits of their tolerance – to know themselves. Cruelty and meanness produce feelings of shame and remorse as bullies and their victims engage in a sado-masochistic dance; you can't have one without the other. Teenagers like to wind each other up to see how far they can go. It's also fun. They create riveting scenarios in the humdrum boredom of their daily lives as the intricacies of who's said what or fallen out with whom. These ongoing dramas become the thrilling soap of daily life and girls love to inject emotional intensity into how they relay that information – 'I couldn't believe she could say that!' Something happens when you bitch and fall out or get upset. You really feel something. You also have to exercise coping strategies and build resilience as a result. 'We can't really talk properly about things to resolve situations and we like the whole drama of it,' says Beth. 'It's a way of getting attention and there's so much that's going on that makes you angry that you need to release it on somebody else.'

The trouble is that so often, the emotional wounds that teenage girls inflict on each other cut deep. Many say that being punched would hurt less. Sticks and stones may break your bones, but silly words enter deep into your consciousness, make you question your sense of self-worth and isolate you from the rest of your peers, for days and weeks and sometimes months. 'Something happened at my old school and this rumour was started by this one person who decided to get me and all these different stories went around and none of them were true but when I said they weren't true people thought it was me who was lying. I ended up leaving the school because of it, and self-harming,' says Anita, who is fifteen, from Manchester. 'We used to be like really good friends and then she turned on me, I don't know why. She didn't really have any of her own friends and she's ended up with a baby now so she has her own issues to deal with. The ones that bitch have their own problems and they'll have problems when they're older.'

Anita ended up happier in another school but the wounds clearly still hurt. When girls are accused of things they didn't do, or of lying and being attention seekers, they are marooned, isolated and alone. They cannot fight back or re-establish themselves without drawing attention once again to their 'crime' or opening themselves up to more accusations of lying or attention seeking. Martha, the fifteen-year-old who found herself suddenly ostracised from the gang for taking off her clothes at a party after having suffered extraordinary stress at home with abuse from her ex-stepfather puts it this way, 'With most girls – say there's one girl and they all don't like her – she could turn round and say something that's totally true, she could say she'd been raped and that was totally true and they'll be like "Oh, she's just attention seeking" and start bitching in front of her, saying all sorts of stuff that just puts her down even more.'

Family

For teenagers there are only two main sources of support and security – home and school. When teenagers have difficulties at home they find it hard not to bring their troubles to school. They either bitch and bully others more in an attempt to feel stronger, or they look to their friends more for support, which can make them even more vulnerable to accusations of attention seeking or lying. Some of the toughest bitches I've met in schools have difficult home lives. They're angry, they get into trouble for fighting and they're full of bravado, joking around pretending that everything is fine. 'I like being a bitch, I don't care what people call me, I am a bitch because I am a bitch, mouthy and slag people off,' says Bonnie from Leeds. The anger from her was palpable. But she was also deeply fragile, the victim of serious abuse at home. Anita from Manchester, who ended up moving to another school and self-harming because of the campaign of rumours spread by a friend, was also having a difficult time at home. 'I used to argue a lot with my mum and then I found out that me dad weren't me real dad but he is me brother and sister's real dad and he'd come and see us at the weekends and try and sort things out between me and me mum and I'd think what's it got to do with you? I ended up running away, I walked all the way to Wolverton and at the same time this girl who was supposed to be my friend was also mouthin' me all the time behind me back. You feel like everything's going wrong for you, there's nowhere else to go, so you run away. If things were better at home you'd feel like you had more people to talk to, to support you and I didn't tell anyone at school about me dad because you can't trust no one you can't trust them not to spread it around. You think going to school will make it better because it'll take your mind off things but it doesn't always work like that. Nothing's easy in school.'

When Lily was having a bad time at home being beaten up and bullied by her brother, her parents failed to take her accusations seriously and her friends didn't believe her. She was accused of being attention seeking rather than supported. 'My parents just got sick of the fighting and said don't come to me so I thought they didn't care and then my friends just said "Why don't you just fight him back?" They didn't believe me. It felt like there wasn't anywhere safe at home because my brother drove me mad and I couldn't sort out my thoughts and I needed more support at school but didn't get it. There was no space to be myself and to try and work things out.' Lily felt so isolated and victimised by girls at school for being gay that she attempted suicide by swallowing twenty-six Paracetemol when she was thirteen. She was taken to hospital and had her stomach pumped. Her parents, well-paid professionals, had refused to take her complaints about being physically assaulted by her brother seriously. The girls at school called her a 'weirdo' and a 'freak'. 'When I got really upset, I was sobbing and shaking all over and felt really sick they just said that it was my best acting performance yet and they still refuse to believe me about what happened with my brother. I just wanted to go to sleep. I thought everything would just be so much easier if I slipped away.'

Emma, the ringleader in the gang of five eleven-year-old girls who turned on Jane and accused her of being bossy, was also having a difficult time at home. When I asked them whether it hurts more to have your family bitched about Emma told me about her younger sister, 'It's been so long since I've seen her. She's only nine and she went to stay for a few days at her Nan's and she didn't come back and that was three years ago. I've seen her about in town but she's not allowed to come to our house. It's like I'm really protective about my family but they can talk about me all they like.'

When teenagers feel their families are under attack, it's an even deeper blow for there is nowhere else to go. You can't talk to your family about what's being said because you don't want to hurt them. 'I have this friend whose mum makes jewellery and this group of girls came up to her and said "God, your mum's a freak, her jewellery is disgusting." It's offensive and it hurts more if it's your family. If it's just you then you can deal with it, but if it's your family you don't know what to say, you can't defend them.' When Bess's parents separated a friend came over after school one day, looked scathingly round at her house and said, 'Oh, when parents split up do you suddenly become poor?' 'I was devastated, it was the most hurtful thing anybody has ever said to me,' says Bess.

When teenagers bitch about a girl's family or her background, they dismantle the very fabric of her being – her status, her roots, her only other source of support. 'When people say bad things about your family then I just feel sick,' says Kirsty, 'I go mad, they haven't done anything wrong. Especially if it's about me mum, then I just punch 'em because she doesn't deserve to be bitched about.' 'It makes me cry when people say horrible things about my family,' says Jemma. Race and disability are now known to be off-limits at many schools, but wealth isn't. 'We know that it is unbelievably cruel to bitch about someone who doesn't have enough money,' says Clare, who goes to an independent school. 'So loads of people bitch about those who do have money, they go "She's *soooo* rich!". Some people get targeted if they spend too much money on something, some girl sees something she's wearing that she likes and asks how much it was. Then she replies, "My God! You've spent *that* much money!" and then other times nobody really cares what it cost but then *you* go and buy the same thing, they tell *you* off for it. Every group has their own rules but then some rules are easier to pass than others.'

The child having a bad time at home tends to react in one of two basic ways at school. She either gets bitchier in an attempt to shore up her own defences and deflect attention from her own vulnerability or she finds ways of attracting attention. When I was at primary school, I was miserable. My parents had divorced and fought continuously over access and alimony. At school I was 'friends' with three popular, pretty girls who kept me just close enough to let me believe I was part of the gang, yet also kept me at arm's length to make sure I knew I wasn't their equal. I made up stories to try and get them to like me. I did whatever they asked (throwing away their apple cores at playtime, funny how that particular task sticks in the mind) and remember two distinct extremes – the joy of being included and invited to play at their houses and the utter misery of feeling excluded, because there was nowhere else to go. They knew I lied to get their attention and accused me of making up stories and each time it happened my status seemed to shrink, yet still I went on doing it. I understood what Lily meant when she said, 'It hurts at the time but if they're bitching about me it's almost empowering, they notice you.'

Once a child has endured this level of exclusion and ostracism she never forgets it. And it resurfaces most vividly when we become parents and watch our own children falling out with their friends. For me the hurt resurfaced when my youngest daughter was eleven and coping with a prolonged row with a girl who had decided to hone in on my daughter as her main rival and enemy. She said nasty things and was intent upon turning my daughter's friends against her and my daughter was in tears regularly. I reassured her as best I could and told her to remember how unhappy this girl must be whenever my daughter felt hurt by her. I did nothing to intervene, which in retrospect was probably not a good idea. I kept it together for the best part of two terms, and when she left the school, I congratulated myself on the fact that we had got away without a major row. Then one sunny afternoon in the summer holidays when we were playing a game of football on Hampstead Heath my daughter got a text from a friend saying they were all in Pizza Express for this girl's birthday. My daughter hadn't been invited, but she didn't need to know that. She dissolved into tears once again and two terms of repressed rage erupted in me. Rather than confronting the issue calmly months ago I had suppressed my own emotions, my own hurt on her behalf to such an extent that I got so upset by this one small thing that

I ended up rowing with another girl's mother – she wasn't even the bitch's mother. It was more painful for me than it was for my daughter. While she was upset, she had a much happier home life than I had had, she didn't need these 'friends' as much as I had needed mine but the event had touched such a raw nerve of emotion that I had confused her needs with my own.

Why You Should Speak Out

Many of the greatest and funniest bitches in this book felt a deep insecurity born of their home life. The American writer Dorothy Parker's mother died of a wasting disease when she was five years old and the young Dorothy always felt she was somehow to blame for it. She hated her stepmother, 'I didn't call her anything, "Hey, you" was the best I could manage' and then when the stepmother died suddenly of a brain haemorrhage, Dorothy felt as if she had two murders on her conscience. Über-screen-bitch Bette Davis had a cold father who she could never please and her arch rival Joan Crawford never really knew her father. Family really matters to children and there is a great deal that parents can do to lighten the load for their daughters.

All childhood traumas seem to go deep into a person's DNA and influence the type of adult they become. When girls are bitched about and isolated they feel the deep searing hurt of humiliation, they lose self-respect and confidence because it is considered so normal, it's hard not to believe that they are in some respects to blame. And when women start blaming themselves, when they turn inwards to try and improve themselves and make themselves more loveable, thinner, more attractive with cooler clothes, they set themselves up for yet more disappointment, failure and vulnerability to depressive syndromes. When girls are bitched about they learn not to trust other girls. As the bully extends twigs of tenderness for her to cling to, leading her on with the false hope of friendship, the powerful pattern of an abusive relationship is established. The victim doesn't dare extricate herself, doesn't know how to stand up for herself and risks being attracted to abusive relationships with men as an adult. The 'bitch' may seem untouched, but she loses out too. Others see how she behaves and fear her. When a bitch's behaviour is not challenged by teachers or parents, they enter a moral universe of their own, stifling empathy of concern for others, where it is fine to do whatever we need to get what we want. Unchallenged bitches learn the age-old feminine wile of manipulation for personal gain and visibility but they lose the trust and respect of other women, the very people we depend on most for the lasting support and friendship that enables us to get through life, as women.

Parents often feel in a dilemma as to how to help their daughters when they are having difficult times with their friends. It can be hard to know when it is appropriate to intervene and when it's best to let them sort out their own problems. Karen is fifteen and believes it should always be left alone, 'It's definitely up to you to sort it. Having other people involved just makes it worse because there's always going to be secrets and next week there'll just be something else, some other "issue" going on.' In some ways she is right. But Karen is strong, confident, sorted and has never been at the receiving end of a concerted campaign. Social ostracism, being repeatedly taunted or accused of things they haven't done is hugely stressful for people of all ages. The stress triggers biological changes to the immune and the cardiovascular system, and if this stress is repeated often enough it can make people ill. If you're being adversely affected by remarks, if your school work is being affected, if it makes you feel tearful and withdrawn, then it requires action. Everyone has different levels of sensitivity and teenagers are often hypersensitive compared to adults. Parents cannot accurately gauge your stress levels by comparing your experiences with what they could tolerate when they also have the benefits of experience and hindsight. Children need to toughen up as they grow up but too often adults endorse cruelty by telling them to ignore the taunts of others. 'They say I'm oversensitive and I have to toughen up,' says Lily, 'but why should I have to? Why hurt me in the first place?'

There is a huge difference between the odd humiliating, catty remark and the drip drip constancy of a campaign of bitching designed to bring someone to their knees. Both are common in schools, but it's the concerted ostracism which is bullying and should be labelled as such. It's not 'just what girls do', it can ruin lives, and girls who find themselves targeted as victims need as much adult help as they can get. When teenagers are in distress they can spiral downwards very quickly without parents noticing. All too often parents under-react to eating disorders, depression, self-harm, drink and drug use because teenagers are very good at hiding these things and parents cannot believe that their own children might be at risk. The same is true of Bitchland. Acknowledging that a young person is suffering and needs greater support does not mean that parents are bad. Life is full of problems and good parents help their children to deal with them by putting their needs rather than their own pride first.

The stronger a girl's sense of self, the more able she will be to deal with the stresses of growing up and Bitchland. When teenagers are aware of their strengths, when they know that they are good at music, dancing or football, they can latch onto those strengths when they feel their confidence threatened in other areas. When social and emotional issues are discussed openly at home from early childhood, teenagers absorb those messages and have resources to draw on when they feel vulnerable socially. With a strong sense of self comes self-belief. 'When people say you're really stupid, you're not right in the head, that can make you feel really down,' says Marisha. 'Ignoring it is not going to sort it, you have to believe it yourself. Your friends say to you "You're not fat," or "You're dead pretty" and they make you feel better for a bit but unless you believe it yourself once you're on your own or something happens, it's all there again.'

Most girls grow out of Bitchland, wounded but wiser. Teenagers are embroiled in a painful process of socialisation as they grow up and once they have developed a firmer sense of self and self-confidence, once they move out of the dense, stressful environment of school and find lovers and friends from other walks of life, they bitch less. 'It's got a lot better now that we're doing GCSEs,' says Kirsty. 'When we were fourteen we all used to bitch about each other like mad but now, we still bitch but now we've got to the point where if someone is pissing you off you can tell them and still be mates.' And then as adults we learn greater restraint and tact. 'We all say things about other people every day and I'd just die if I heard someone saying those things about me,' says Elizabeth Noble, 'but does that make me mean? At fourteen I would probably have actually said it to their faces but now I wouldn't dream of it, I know better.'

I consider telling my brother, asking him for help. But tell him what exactly? I have no black eyes, no bloody noses to report: Cordelia does nothing physical. If it was boys, chasing or teasing, he would know what to do, but I don't suffer from boys in this way. Against girls and their indirectness, their whisperings, he would be helpless.

From *Cat's Eye* by Margaret Atwood

Top Bitch Reading For Teens

by Amanda Craig

Strong girls have always been around in children's books and stories, but up until the 1960s you had to know where to look for them. One of my favourite fairy tales is 'Molly Whuppie', a Scottish version of 'Jack the Giant-Killer'. Cast out with her two sisters by their parents, Molly escapes four times from a wicked giant and his wife and wins half the kingdom and the king's son as a result. In exchange for a husband for herself and each of her sisters, she steals the giant's three most precious possessions (his sword, his purse and his ring), one by one. When the giant catches her and is about to kill her, Molly cleverly suggests he tie her up in a bag and go into the wood to cut the biggest stick he can find. While he's doing this, she tricks the giant's wife into climbing into the bag in her place.

Molly is clever, determined, brave and active – the opposite of the passive, sleepy or suffering heroines we associate with fairy tales. But although there are other strong girls around, from Mossycoat to the brave lassie of *East O' the Sun, West O' the Moon*, children's novelists have taken a while to rediscover them. One of the first, and best, is Mary in Frances Hodgson Burnett's *The Secret Garden*. Mary is so plain and sulky that other children call her 'Mary, Mary quite contrary.' Friendless and orphaned, she needs every drop of bad temper when she goes to live with her uncle at Mistlethwaite Manor on the Yorkshire moors. It is her restive boredom that pushes her to restore the secret garden, and her appalling temper that empowers her to stand up to her spoilt, sickly cousin instead of bending to his will. Although Mary becomes gentler and prettier (strange how those two attributes go together) she never quite loses her prickliness, and fierceness, and, as a junior version of Jane Eyre, it's what you love her for.

Jo in *Little Women* lacks any trace of the malign, but she, too, is a strong girl. Clumsy, impulsive, energetic and perilously outspoken, she is by far the most interesting of the March sisters, and the engine of all their adventures. You never forgive Louisa M. Alcott for not marrying Jo to Laurie in *Good Wives*, but by making Jo a writer, supporting the whole family, she gives us one of the first portraits in children's literature of a woman surviving by her own wits and energy.

Roberta in E. Nesbit's *The Railway Children* is similarly proactive. She loses her temper and makes her irritating younger brother almost faint playing a game, but it is Roberta who stays behind in the dark railway tunnel with a wounded schoolboy, and Roberta who discovers the truth about their missing father and who sets in motion the events that save her father when he is unjustly imprisoned. Similarly, Anthea in the *Five Children and It* trilogy is the one who not only persuades the waspish sand-fairy to give them one more wish but has the moral courage to confront unpleasant adults and get them to change their ways (with a bit of magical assistance). The ideal big sister, Nesbit's heroines are hugely important because they show girls that if they are determined, brave and resourceful they can change their world. They have their direct descendent in Harry Potter's friend Hermione, 'the cleverest witch of her generation', who is fearlessly bookish but also bold enough to punch Malfoy and outwit a werewolf.

All these strong girls have the advantage of starting off in nice, clean, middle-class families. One of my favourite heroines in literature has none of these. She is Dido Twite, the guttersnipe daughter of a family of treasonous crooks who makes her first appearance in *Black Hearts in Battersea*, the second of Joan Aiken's twelve-volume *Wolves of Willoughby Chase* series. Dido is a cheeky, half-starved waif ignored by all until Simon the painter arrives in London and befriends her. In return for a few crumbs of kindness, Dido saves Simon's life when he gets kidnapped – apparently at the cost of her own, for while he survives she is lost at sea. Yet it takes more than an ocean to kill Dido, a girl-Odysseus whose long struggle to return home involves confounding conspirators, outfacing witches and injecting spirit into various passive, terrified girls. Outrageously cheeky, with many rude phrases of her own invention, Dido is dirty, rebellious and brave in a way that makes her the undoubted ancestor of Philip Pullman's Lyra in *His Dark Materials*.

Jacqueline Wilson's Tracy Beaker is another girl from the rough side. Taken into a children's home because her mum's monstrous boyfriend beat her up, she is violent and rude but longs for her mother to come and take her away. The book consists of her thoughts, fantasies and feelings as a troubled but affectionate ten-year-old who may never be rescued by an adult, whether this is the adoptive parents she has antagonised, the glamorous mother who has dumped her, or the writer, Cam, who befriends her. Tracy makes you laugh and cry, though in real life you'd probably dislike her as a bully.

Lyra Belacqua in *His Dark Materials* is the greatest of all bitch heroines. Passionate, imperious and brave she first gets into trouble trying to rescue her best friend, Roger, who gets kidnapped by the evil Mrs Coulter. She learns to read the aleithiometer, or truth-compass, helps the huge armoured bear Iorek Byrnisson win back his kingdom, releases other kidnapped children before they can meet a fate worse than death and, with the help of Will in the second and third book of the trilogy, brings down God Himself. Her fierce will, loyalty and self-aggrandising lies all make you fall in love with her even if at times you (and the author) laugh at her, too. Like Sally Lockhart, the Victorian detective from Pullman's earlier quartet, she is someone you'd definitely want on your side in a fight.

I strongly suspect all these heroines are inspired by Gerda and the Robber Maiden in Hans Christian Andersen's *The Snow Queen*, not least because so many seem to encounter evil in the frozen North. Lucy in C.S. Lewis's *The Lion, the Witch and the Wardrobe* is unfortunately just a bit too good to be a serious opponent to the Empress Jadis, but later on Lewis makes a better fist of it with Aravis in *The Horse and His Boy*, and the distinctly stroppy Jill of *The Silver Chair*. Catherine Fisher's Jessa in *The Snow-walker's Son* trilogy is known as 'Two Knives Jessa', and, like Lewis's heroines, travels north to rescue the wicked Gudrun's son and rival, Kari. Anne Halam has Sloe, a girl exiled in Siberia with her mother, who is the secret guardian of the tiny Lindqvists – the last 'seeds' of all remaining wild animals in the world. Crippled and viciously courageous, Sloe makes her way across 1000 miles of ice and snow to save the animals and find her mother again in an enthralling fusion of fairytale and science fiction. Other wonderful heroines include N.M. Browne's Ursula in *Warriors of Alavna*, Renn in Michelle Paver's *Chronicles of Ancient Darkness* and Kitty in Jonathan Stroud's *Bartimaeus* trilogy, who are fearsome adversaries. The fighting heroine has even made her appearance in Cressida Cowell's hilarious books about the Viking nerd Hiccup, in the form of Kamikaze, the small daughter of the terrifying Big Boobied Bertha (who suffocates her victims between her breasts.)

What is strange about these heroines is that, despite appearing more and more frequently in children's literature, they are still pretty sparse in adult novels. For every V.I. Warshawski in the Molly Whuppie mould, there are far too many passive, romantic heroines who are direct descendents of Cinderella and Sleeping Beauty – with the result that, in terms of self-confidence, literary heroines have actually gone backwards since the days of Jane Eyre. It's ironic that girls get told they can be strong and self-determined as children, only to have the rug swept from under their feet as soon as they grow up.

~

Amanda Craig is the author of five novels, and the children's books critic of *The Times*. Her website, which includes recommended reading for children aged one to twelve, is www.amandacraig.com.

How Your Parents Can Help

- Often the last person you want to talk to about problems with friends and school is your parents. But the chances are pretty high that if you're upset or angry about something, they will have noticed. The anxieties of loving parents can be immense. They really care about you and jump to all sorts of imaginative conclusions when they don't know what is really going on. If you feel that you can cope with your friendship problems on your own – tell them. Describe what's going on in the broadest terms so that they don't worry about you unduly.

- Don't fall into the trap of thinking that you *have* to cope with this all alone. Parents will have all sorts of takes, expertise and wisdom about social situations simply because they are so old. They will be able to offer you a different perspective. It really helps sometimes to be able to sound off with someone who understands and has your best interests at heart.

- If your parents are likely to overreact and immediately want to storm into the school and see the head, ring another girl's mother or move you to another school, preface any conversation with firm guidelines – you don't want them to do anything to make things worse. You just want them to listen.

- Don't let them dismiss your concerns as trivial. If it hurts it's serious.

- If you find talking to your parents difficult, leave this book lying around and see if they pick it up. Take out *Mean Girls* or *Heathers* from the video shop and watch it with them.

- Find another adult to talk to, a family friend or a teacher you feel particularly close to. They won't overreact and will listen. Adults went to school too and every woman understands the nature of the bitch-victim relationship and the way girls become so emotionally embroiled and cruel. Sometimes just knowing that this is normal helps. But that doesn't make it right.

Bitch Etiquette

There is a big difference between being the kind of bitch that is strong, outspoken, wants to be heard more than she wants to be liked and doesn't take any crap from anyone, and the bitch that is rude, cruel and manipulative. The first kind of bitch is what every woman should aspire to be, for it is the only way to ensure that you will live life to the full and get your just desserts. Strong bitches ooze self-confidence from every pore, they don't need to proclaim fake confidence constantly by putting others down. Strong bitches inspire others; weak bitches build tension and insecurity between women. They also run the risk of losing the support of real friends when they most need them. This section of *The Big Fat Bitch Book* will tell you how to limit the weak and hurtful bitch in you and become more confident; how to deflect and withstand hurtful comments if you become the target of a bitching campaign and how to be a better bitch when others are being so unpleasant and stupid that they deserve it.

~

QUIZ
What Kind of Bitch Are You?
(Answers page 87)

- *You are with two good friends at a bus stop. You get on the bus with one friend, leaving the other behind to wait for a different bus. Do you*

a) slag her off the moment the doors are closed behind you
b) make a plan together that excludes the other girl
c) watch other people on the bus and text each other comments, but say nothing much at all, you're much too tired and hungry to talk

- *When someone you would like to be better friends with asks you what you think of another girl who you know she doesn't like, do you*

a) fabricate a juicy story about the girl that will raise her interest and your status
b) pretend you don't like her (when you actually don't have anything against her)
c) say you honestly don't really know much about her

- *How much of your daily conversation involves talking about other people's appearance and sexual conduct (exclude celebrities) –*

a) 85%
b) 50%
c) 10%

- *When a friend asks you if you think she's pretty/clever/ interesting do you*

a) tell her to stop being such a conceited attention seeker
b) say that you think that we're all pretty average in the attraction/intelligence stakes
c) say 'Of course, you are silly'

- *When someone tells you a secret about somebody else you*
  a) immediately cash in on the info and tell the whole school through every possible medium – notes on noticeboards, MSN and a whispering campaign
  b) become incredibly close and supportive to that person, dropping hints that you know that something is wrong but that you want to help her, so that you can find out more
  c) keep it to yourself

- *When you feel insecure about your body do you*
  a) slag off someone else publicly by laughing at what they're wearing or how they've done (or not done) their hair
  b) say 'I'm so fat/ugly/my thighs are like watermelons' so that somebody makes you feel better for five seconds by saying 'If you're fat, I must be obese.'
  c) go through your best friend's wardrobe to try out some more flattering styles

- *You discover that a girl has got off with a boy you fancy. You*
  a) spread a rumour round school that she is pregnant and threw herself at him
  b) drop hints to the boy that the girl is obsessed with him and could start to stalk him
  c) find someone else to fantasise about

- *You've had a bad day. A teacher has told you off in front of the whole class for something you didn't do and lost your home-work, but insists that you never handed it in, plus you've just discovered there's a really good party on Saturday in a free house but you can't go because it's your grandmother's 80th birthday, so you*

a) spread a rumour that the party is off

b) lie to your parents about it being a best friend's birthday and ask if you can leave Gran's early

c) shrug your shoulders, say it can't be helped, hope that tomorrow is a better day and tell yourself that the party will be crap anyway

- *You're with all of your friends except for one – the girl you all find deeply irritating at that moment. The others start to talk about her . . . you*

a) volunteer a particularly humiliating anecdote and laugh your head off

b) listen to what everyone else says, laugh with them but say nothing

c) stand up for her by talking about all her good characteristics

Answers

Mostly a's: You're an alpha bitch and its time to take control of your actions and your tongue if you want to keep your friends *and* go far in life.

Mostly b's: You're bitching is more subtle and sophisticated, but watch out. If you get found out you may lose the trust of those you most admire and need.

Mostly c's: You're a saint, but be careful that others don't turn on you for being too good. It's important to show a little grit and honest hate sometimes.

Controlling Your Inner Bitch

MRS HUBER: Susan, have you been able to find old clothes
for Edie? She has nothing to wear.
SUSAN: I thought that was the look she was going for.
MRS HUBER: Oh Susan, Edie may be trash but she's still a
human being.

Desperate Housewives

'Sometimes you really can't help bitching because there's
something in you that you want to say and you don't want to
say it because it's mean but it just slips out,' says twelve-year-
old Camilla. We all think malicious, slanderous, even
murderous, thoughts about other people because often other
people aren't very nice, or say particularly stupid things. You
don't have to like everybody all of the time. You don't even
have to like anybody, but if we all said exactly what we thought
about each other all of the time, nobody would have any
friends. The more intelligent you are, the more likely you are
to be able to think up amusing, cutting quips and the more
careful you have to be. We all do it, no matter how old you are.
Germaine Greer confessed at a publishers' lunch when the subject of this book came up, 'You know you shouldn't, but
sometimes it just pops out.'

There is great pleasure to be found in witty put-downs. It's fun, cathartic, addictive and essential banter in good mutual friendships. But when you feel that bile rise, when you feel that irresistible urge, that scratch that just has to be itched, pause for just a second to consider your motives. Is this verbal banter between equals? Are they strong enough to take it? Is this a one-off comment or do you always say this to her? Could you tolerate the same from them? Are you angry or jealous of this person, or with someone else entirely, but haven't got the guts to challenge them honestly? Or are you just bored and penned in, surrounded by constant noise and hundreds of others at school?

It's only once you start to understand why you say certain things that you can begin to know yourself better and take control over what you say. There are times when it's important to be able to bitch well – when people put you down needlessly, hurt or betray you, or when they're being intensely irritating or inconsiderate and show no signs of desisting. There are plenty of examples if you turn over and read *The Big Fat Bitch Book For Grown-Up Girls* which you can copy or adapt for your own needs. But when you are young and vulnerable at school, it is important to remember that others are fragile and equally vulnerable. Be honest with yourself. If one person bears the brunt of your bitchery, it's time to button those lips for a while. By taking control over what you say, you will feel better about yourself and exude greater confidence as a result.

'If someone bitches about your friend you feel like it's your duty to say they said this about you,' says fourteen-year-old Holly. But it isn't your duty. As a good friend you should not be doing anything to hurt their feelings. We all know that other people talk about us when we're not there, but we don't need to know what they are saying. So don't repeat what people say about others in your presence, ever. Whether you're a teenager at a sleepover or an adult at a dinner party, gossip is privileged information to that party and should never be related back to the person under discussion. You may feel that the person ought to know, or like to know how much you have defended them as a friend but they will only hear the slander first, not your shock, outrage or loyalty. And if as a gang of girls you are having a bitch about someone else, don't assume that you are entirely innocent just because you don't join in. By remaining silent, you condone nastiness; by making a stand and speaking out against it you assert individuality and strength.

A joke is only a joke if everyone enjoys it. If it's at another's expense and they find it hard to laugh too then it's a bitch too far. Try not to make bitchy comments on email, MSN or by text because it is much harder to grasp any irony intended from the tone (because there isn't any) and words can easily be misinterpreted. When you're with people you can push the limits that much more, sensing when you might have offended someone or gone too far and then apologise immediately and unreservedly. Don't laugh it off with 'Joke. Can't you take a joke? That's doubly bitchy, implying that they are not strong enough to take it. Discussing a scenario ostensibly about someone else but in front of the person (who therefore knows it is actually about her) is a common teenage bitch tactic which is also unacceptable. It's bullying, unsubtle and vindictive, alienating an individual who cannot hit back.

Gossipy emails are always dangerous because they can be

forwarded on by malevolent stirrers. If you've got something really important to say, say it out loud or not at all. Whispering is rude, exaggerates the importance of what you're saying and makes others paranoid. Be very careful how you respond to the leading question, 'What do you think of X?' Unless you are 100 per cent confident that this friend is trustworthy, it is wise to hold back any negative observations or information even when they take the lead by bitching first. Never start a sentence with 'No offence, but . . .' because it's obvious to everyone that you are about to say something bitchy. And think about the meaning of some of the words that others use with such abandon.

Girls get put down as 'mean girls' or 'bitches' whenever they do something that others don't like. But when you think about it, these are catch-all put-downs which don't describe people accurately. Real people are never all good or all bad, just a mass of emotional confusion trying their best to get on. If you push others into these stereotypes, you risk being stereotyped yourself. Try to identify and separate out what it is they've done or said that you don't like and talk about those, don't dismiss the whole person. Look at all of their other positive points. The chances are they far outweigh the bad. In the film *Mean Girls*, Maths teacher Ms Norbury (played by Rosalind Wiseman, the author of *Queen Bees and Wannabes*) tells the girls that they have to stop calling each other 'sluts' and 'whores'. 'You just give boys the excuse to call you all those things,' she says. Young men are not called 'sluts', 'bitches', 'whores' or 'dogs'. They're 'womanisers', 'Casanovas' or 'sexy', 'fit' and 'buff' in a positive way. You're not actually a 'slut' if you snog someone at a party, you just snogged someone at a party. 'Sluts' sleep around, 'whores' sell their bodies for sex – but men are never insulted with these terms. And aren't girls just as entitled to explore their sexuality at their own pace as boys? How many of the girls that get called these words fit the dictionary definition? These are powerful, damaging insults and once any news gets passed around school with the word 'slut' anywhere in the sentence, the word sticks. You give girls a reputation, you push girls into becoming that stereotype and you bring all women down by perpetuating the double standard. If we question the negative female stereotypes that are liberally tossed out about women we learn to use them less in everyday speech. When you feel the urge to call someone else a 'slut' or a 'whore', what is it that you really dislike about their behaviour? Are you jealous because you fancied the same boy and weren't brave enough to go for him? Or do you just wish you could be a bit more brave with boys in general? A happy sex life is every young woman's right, and for most of us it's a long and often tricky road to any sort of happiness or sexual fulfilment. Girls have just as much of a right to sexual experimentation as boys. Gaining sexual experience should not make anyone feel cheap.

All those little meannesses that we can't resist do not in the end make us feel any happier. They make us feel guilty and bad about ourselves at a time in our lives when we most need to muster every possible resource in order to feel good. We assume bitchery as a means of defence and to distinguish ourselves as powerful, but in actual fact it just makes us more vulnerable to isolation and retaliation as others grow wary. True leadership, good leadership emerges when people are calm and non-judgemental, when they can arbitrate between warring parties because they are considered fair and trusted. True leaders are democratic, able to accept differences of opinion, not autocratic bullies. And if we are to succeed and achieve our ambitions as girls in a world where the odds are stacked against us, we need to develop these skills. We all want to feel that we are accepted by other people and have influence. Finding the strength to be tolerant and kind is a good start. And one final word of warning . . . meanness can be extremely dangerous for the appearance. Over time the face grows pinched, the eyes narrow and become nervy and distrustful. You will end up with the face you deserve, Bitch!

It's fine to bitch so long as they don't find out. They probably know you're bitching about them and they're probably bitching about you, just don't do it in a mean way which is often more to do with the tone than with what you're actually saying. It's just something to talk about.

Alice, fourteen

~

Don't whisper, it arouses suspicion. If you stand around and talk normally you're more likely not to be noticed.

Camilla, twelve

~

In our class there are loads of groups and it's fine so long as you make sure you keep it in your group and tell only your friends. We also have a bitching corner and you can go there and sit and talk and no one comes over because they know we're just having a bitch to let off steam.

Francesca, fifteen

~

You can bitch in quite a nice way sometimes. There's this girl who's never sworn in her whole life so when we talk about her it's about that and when you think about it, that's actually a good thing.

Clare, twelve

Hannah and Bess (both fifteen) say:

- Be generous
- Present yourself well, look good
- Don't bitch about people if you don't want to be bitched about – they'll find out
- Listen and be understanding
- You've gotta be popular
- You've gotta contribute and make jokes to the group
- If someone says 'She's being such a bitch' or something negative about another friend you can't agree with her and its best not to get involved. Laugh and say 'OK' or dissipate the conversation by saying 'there, there' but don't take it any further or make your opinion heard

- Don't overstep the mark, stay within your own comfort level of nastiness
- Be careful about what you say to sensitive people. You've gotta know the other person's bitching limits. With me [Hannah] you could say 'She looks like a fucking dog' and I'd just laugh but if you said that to someone else they could be really hurt

Top Tips for Teenagers

I asked Rosalind Wiseman for her top tips. They are:

- Make a pledge not to gossip for half an hour a day, at a time when you usually gossip a lot like dinner time, waiting for the bus or walking together. That way you get to understand how much of our talk is bitchy gossip. We just think of it as talking, but actually it's only when it's not about you that you assume it's talking.

- If you can't change the subject, try and find something positive to say about them. You don't have to be lovey-dovey friends but there must be something good about them

- If you have a friend who is always bitching about others, tell her what you don't like about the way she talks when you are alone together. Say how much you value her as a friend but that 'You're better than this.' I'm always saying that to girls – 'You're better than this . . .'

- If someone is bitching about someone else just say 'I don't know if its true but even if it is true, so what?'

- When kids tell me that they have no choice but to bitch because everybody else does I say 'What sort of a woman do you want to be? Powerful, the sort that gets stuff done? Well then, look who's making the decisions for you. How much do you want to be in control of your life? It's your choice, you can choose to do the right thing. You can do it.'

Calling somebody else fat won't make you any skinnier. Calling someone stupid doesn't make you any smarter. And ruining Regina George's life definitely didn't make me any happier. All you can do in life is try to solve the problem in front of you.

Cady in *Mean Girls*

We Are Beautiful, No Matter What They Say, Words Can't Bring Us Down

People say a lot of things they usually don't mean. Verbose garbage just comes out of their mouths and if they were to hear a day's worth of their own conversation played back to them on tape they would be deeply bored and appalled. Recognising this universal human weakness is the first step to building resilience. After you've taken essential exchanges of information out of the equation – Have you seen my mobile/It's Mum's birthday on Sunday and I haven't got any money for a present/There's a major diversion on the bus route home – most of the rest of what people say is just rubbish. When someone says something which could be interpreted the wrong way, always give them the benefit of the doubt, they probably didn't mean it to be hurtful. Words are just letters in a row. Ignore them.

When we feel vulnerable, insecure, fat, unattractive, unloved and unlovable we are much more sensitive to what people say. Even 'How are you?' or 'Have you lost weight?' can be interpreted as an aggressive question. Understanding how

our sensitivities interact with what's being said to us is essential
if we're not to make things worse or intimate friendship difficult. It's important to be able to stand back from what people
say and assess it unemotionally. Is this affectionate teasing
between mutual friends or an indirect insult from someone
who bears a grudge or doesn't like me? If it's the former laugh
it off, express fake indignation or match like with like. Is this
the first time she's said this or have there been other veiled
comments, which indicate that something else is going on?
Don't run crying to others about how horrible she's being, that
will only make you appear more of a victim. Perhaps there are
difficulties in 'the bitch's' life that you don't know about. Just
saying to someone 'What's up with X, she's being a bit sharp
today,' may be enough to explain a great deal. If you suspect
there's something more personal going on, a hidden hostility
between the two of you, then ask them directly if you have
done something to offend them. Put them on the spot in an
unemotional manner when you are alone, so that she can be
honest without losing face in front of others. Try and clear the
air rather than swallowing the insult and allowing that grudge
to grow. 'You can feel it when someone's talking about you
behind your back,' says Amanda, who is fifteen. 'If you say to
one of them "I heard you talking about me" it kind of diffuses
the whole thing and you then feel like you've taken the power
back.'

If someone insults your prowess at something you know
you're not very good at, don't take offence, agree with them
and then say what you are good at. 'I am crap at doing cart-
wheels but I can make a mean pavlova' and then pay them a
compliment about how good they are at the particular skill

they've trashed in you. That was what they were looking for in the first place. Don't do yourself down or negate your own skills before you've even started with phrases such as, 'I'm crap at tennis/swimming/cooking/maths.' You only give others licence to put you down if you don't value yourself. Don't negate compliments either. If someone says you look nice, or admires your skirt say 'Thanks, I like it too' not 'Oh, its just a really cheap old scrap of a thing.' Confidence comes from within but even the most confident woman has to fake it sometimes. If you show others that you value yourself they are more likely to value you too.

Hold back anecdotes and personal information until you're fairly certain you can trust that person. Be careful who you give your phone number or password out to, particularly when you start at a new secondary school. When you start at a new school you want everybody to be your friend, but often those you thought were nice turn out to be people you have nothing in common with once you get to know them and grow a little older. And be careful not to drop old friends even though you may find yourself under pressure from other new friends to do so. We need as many friends as we can get, from all walks of life, and as we get older it is often the friends who had stood by us the longest that we need and value the most. If you find yourself at the receiving end of a consistent campaign of bitching at school with all the added frills – the silent treatment, rumours, a general feeling of being shunned by people you considered your friends – you need to practice defensive strategies and develop a second skin so that you can screen out all of the things that you don't need to hear and focus on the many strengths that you have. When someone is determined to abuse you they will have their own reasons for doing so. Being thinner, prettier, kinder is not going to make them change. Strong self-esteem comes from knowing yourself, not from how others perceive you.

Growing a Second Skin

Body language says a great deal. Stand tall with an open body posture, don't cross your arms defensively. Smile and practise looking confident in front of a mirror. Don't make it easy for others to pick on you. Practise your replies, as if you were going on a date, and make it funny if you can, humour disarms. Modify some of the examples in this book to fit the situation. The bully wastes a great deal of time thinking about your weaknesses to be able to pick on them so accurately. What are their weaknesses? They must have deep insecurities to feel the need to pick on you. Focus on their vulnerabilities and feel sorry for them. You are unique, special, strong. Make a list of all your strengths on one side of the page, and their weaknesses on the other. Keep two diaries, one for the good, another for the bad. It may well be that once you look back over what has been said and done it seems less frequent or severe than you had first thought. Write down all of the upsetting things that have been said on a piece of paper and set fire to it. When people say hurtful things they aim for the core of your being. If you choose not to believe them, if you question the reasoning behind their insults and remember that people hit out to make themselves feel bigger, if you focus on your own list of personal strengths and assets, you protect that core. Hitting like with like can be demeaning and strong people are supposed to be able to rise above it. But it's wise to keep a few clever put-downs up your sleeve for when you're really cornered. 'When someone says something horrible to your face it does help to say something back to them. They might not apologise, but it makes you feel better,' says Deborah, who is fourteen.

When someone bitches about the way you look, don't say anything rude back, just smile, say 'Thanks for the compliment' sarcastically and focus intensely on their thighs, or some other less-than-perfect body part of their own and imagine it exploding. The power of imagination is strong. Imagine the bitch becoming prey to all sorts of nasty mishaps – run over by a bus like Regina George in *Mean Girls*, left alone in the heart of the jungle with nothing but snakes and leeches for company, or mysteriously covered in large boils. Smile sweetly and blow her a kiss as you think these mean thoughts. Thinking nasty thoughts will not make them happen, but they will make you feel a great deal better. Develop your own personal and very private mantra, which you can repeat over and over when you feel compromised by other bitches or teachers intent on giving you a hard time.

Sixteen-year-old Tessa made a mistake with some permanent hair dye. 'How long will it last?' asked her boyfriend nervously. He clearly didn't like it. 'Probably longer than you will' came back the reply. If you have a physical weakness that you feel vulnerable about – funny shaped ears, over-bleached hair – think of a witty comment, some way to mock yourself mildly before someone else sticks the knife in deeper – 'I'm thinking of going for a part in *Sesame Street*'/'My mum says she could turn me over and use me as a floor mop'/'Eat your heart out, don't you all want calves like these?' If you put yourself down in a humorous way you make others feel a bit more relaxed about their own physical insecurities. But make sure you don't do it in such a way that could be interpreted by someone as fishing for compliments – the age-old trick of saying 'I'm so fat' so that you get the reply 'No you're not (when actually she's thinking 'If she thinks she's fat then I must be obese'), because that could easily backfire with the reply 'Well, you said it.' We're usually made to feel unattractive by other women, not by men. The male sex craves adoration from any female and struts his stuff like a peacock. So while good looks may seem paramount to a girl when it comes to attracting someone, when anybody begins to get to know you, they quickly see through the veneer to your other qualities – to your wit, your warmth and your astute intelligence. A confident smile and a subtle sense of humour weaves far more magic than a pretty face in any social situation.

Intellectual put-downs can be equally hurtful. If someone says 'Haven't you even *heard* of Bob Dylan?' or 'Don't you know what "solipsism" means?' don't pretend that you do know because you'll only get tested and exposed further as a liar. Bat it back with something sarcastic like 'Well I bet knowing that makes all the difference to your life' and then walk away. Don't stay in the presence of someone intent on putting you down. Their aim is to whittle away your confidence but they can only succeed if you stay there and let them. Powerful people like to exude a magnetism, they depend upon an entourage and while it can be hard to pull yourself away because you crave their friendship and that affirmation, ultimately you will only gain by proving your strength and remember that as Eleanor Roosevelt once famously said, 'No one can make you feel inferior without your consent.'

Sorry Seems to be the Hardest Word

When apologies are genuine they can melt a mountain of hostility, but all too often we say 'sorry' when we don't really mean it and would willingly repeat the insult given half the chance. Parents inculcate the notion of saying 'sorry' as often as 'please' or 'thank you' from an early age. The implication is that an apology alone will make amends – wrongs are suddenly righted, meanness or cruelty evaporates. When small children are made to say sorry without understanding why what they did was wrong, they learn an important lesson – that you can carry on being as mean and nasty as you like provided you apologise or nobody sees. The word comes out as 'so . . . r . . r . . y' making it quite clear that they aren't at all. 'People say sorry when they see I'm upset,' says Lily, who is fifteen, 'but I've been apologised to so many times and then someone does something else to upset me a couple of weeks later. They just say sorry to get me off their backs. People react to what they see on the surface, not to what you might be feeling underneath.'

An apology is not an admission of weakness, although it can feel like that. 'If you apologise to someone face-to-face or say "Why did you hurt me?" it's as if you're admitting defeat,' says fourteen-year-old Holly. The most important thing about an apology is not who is right or wrong or an admission of guilt. Why would anyone want to do that? When we apologise we extend the hand of kindness to another human being, we say that we value the relationship in spite of our differences and that we all make mistakes. The resulting emotion of shame is nothing to be ashamed of either. By feeling bad about something we have said or done we add strings to our moral conscience and recognise where the potential limits of our worst attributes really lie. We're allowed to make mistakes and learn from them particularly when we're young, but it can be difficult to know how or when to apologise. It's hard then to find a way to jump in and say sorry before it's too late. Bess still feels bad about being accidentally bitchy to a friend. 'I was wearing her jeans and they were really baggy on me and then when I saw her wearing them the next time I said "How come they're tight on you and baggy on me?" It just came out as a fact without me realising. I didn't mean it to be spiteful and she just went quiet and I'd hate it if someone said that to me. But I didn't apologise, I just sort of tried to make out that it hadn't happened at all and she didn't say anything either.'

It's never too late to apologise when you really mean it. Sometimes it's better after the event because the emotions are less volatile. It shouldn't be embarrassing or shameful either. Admitting that you made a mistake puts you in a position of strength, you lance animosity effectively and enhance your own reputation with others for having done the right thing. But you have to do it in the right way. Laughing it off as a joke, or saying 'I'm sorry you took it that way,' is not an apology at all. Mumbling 'sorry' as you look shiftily at the ground and then move on is not going to do much to build bridges, in fact it could make things even worse. What matters is how the insult was received, not how it was intended.

Never apologise by email or text because the words easily get misinterpreted. It's cowardly and they won't feel your regret in the tone of your voice. Bringing up past grievances won't help either. Don't say 'I'm sorry but you did provoke me by . . . and you still haven't paid me back for . . .' Take complete responsibility for the mistake and make sure you don't apologise for the wrong thing, for something that is less grievous. Look straight at the person and apologise wholeheartedly. And don't make your apology all about you, expressing your own regret and the need to feel less guilty. The most successful apologies work because the recipient feels vindicated, because she feels you understand her pain. Even the biggest bitch can regain the higher ground by apologising properly. You feel better for having cleared the air and you lance the possibility of defensive strikes.

If you are being apologised to by a bitch, accept it with good grace. Listen to what they say and thank them for apologising. Don't bring up past grudges (they're not apologising for their whole life but for one action or mistake) or make unnecessary demands, which might make them feel guiltier. If this is only a momentary gesture of conciliation you will soon know, in which case you have to decide how many apologies you are prepared to accept before you have nothing more to do with them.

Nobody is all good or all bad. The world is not divided into bullies and victims. We're all capable of getting angry, of being mean and behaving thoughtlessly or aggressively towards others. You don't have to like someone else all of the time just because she's a girl, or popular, or good-looking, rich and famous with a lovely husband and two edibly attractive children (bitch). Being female doesn't mean that you always have to maintain the fiction that you care more about others than you do about yourself. Women are particularly bad at apology and forgiveness. We have a tendency to apologise too quickly, when we're still angry and don't really mean it, and we pretend to forgive because we would rather avoid the dialogue that comes from confrontation all together. If you're not sorry, if you don't care enough about the other person, if you've had a fight with someone and said mean things to someone who has behaved really badly towards you and shows no sign of apology, remorse or of maturing into a proper human being, if an apology isn't going to change anything, don't bother. Just walk away, Renée. At least then you both know exactly where you stand.

Anger is an Energy

There are a great many things to get angry about. The daily minutiae of life – getting up, finding a clean pair of socks and dealing with the swathes of irritating people like parents and teachers is bad enough. When it comes to the frustrations associated with all of the bigger issues, such as finding a place as an economically viable adult in the world, you are understandably fit to burst. There is huge pressure over exams, results and the competitive nature of university entrance. There are difficult decisions to make about what you want to do with your life. There's never enough money to buy the things you want, like those skinny jeans that look so fucking good on her (bitch). And as we grow older, we grow wiser to the inequities of this world, where boys can do better just because they are boys and girls need to be attractive and duplicitous if they want to succeed; presenting that kind, feminine veneer to a heart of steely determination and ambition.

Girls get just as angry as boys, it's a natural human emotion, but it is harder for us to express that anger in healthy ways. It's considered inappropriate. So we absorb that rage, blame ourselves for not being strong enough to cope with what life chucks at us and then when we feel the anger at life bubbling up inside us, we release it by bitching about others. Repressed anger can lead to depression and anxiety, eating disorders and self-harm. And girls who learn how to repress their anger grow into women who hold negative emotions in for so long that they become explosive and vengeful when they can't take it any more.

So let it out, girls. Get angry when things make you mad and then feel better. Go somewhere private and shout. Punch pillows and walls. You're not weak and pathetic when you get cross, just human, because there's enough aggravating shit in daily life to turn the most placid doormat into a mass murderer. But be honest with yourself about what's really making you angry – are you just bitching off steam at some poor girl who happens to be a little plump and wearing clashing colours because you feel seriously pissed off about the pressure to look good and not eat when all you want to do is cram 600 Topics into your mouth? When a friend or boyfriend is being particularly demanding, irritating and attention seeking don't just bitch about them being tiresome and difficult to others, consider why they are being like this. Find space to talk with them about their problems. And row with them. Rowing, good old fashioned argument where views are expressed and considered and either accepted or rejected, is how we learn to accept differences in people and forge even greater closeness.

There is a big difference between expressing anger, which is a normal natural emotion, and physical or verbal aggression (bitching), which is offensive and illegal as in 'Assault' or 'Slander'. When anger isn't expressed in healthy ways, it mutates into aggression. Sometimes we feel angry enough to smash things or hit people but most of the time something stops us, a moral respect for others as well as the knowledge from past experience that you rarely win by losing control. Sometimes I get so consumed by road rage that I could drive my car wilfully straight into the side of the car that's just cut me up – but that wouldn't solve anything, just hurt me and my car. By shouting or swearing in private, engaging in competitive sports where you are allowed to vent your frustration or simply by punching a cushion, we let out our rage in more positive ways and we stop ourselves from venting that aggression on others in more criminal ways. We can exercise the same restraint, the same secondary responses with verbal aggression. Just because we think something, doesn't mean we have to say it, and without that self-control, sometimes we let it all splurge out and hurt people without meaning to. Smile and grip those lips, even though you want to spit.

If you feel you're about to lose it with someone, walk away and try and cool down. Try and pinpoint why they have made you feel so angry and then instead of bitching about them to others, find a quiet moment to confront them. Women can be incredibly bad at telling people how they really feel. We expect others to just know why we're upset, to be able to read our minds and then we get even more upset when they fail to even notice. We shy away from honest and direct confrontation with friends, family and lovers because we fear the consequences. But you can get angry with people in positive ways which will improve your relationships, strengthening the bond in those weakest spots. It is possible to get angry with someone and not lose love. Often it is the knowledge that other women are being dishonest that provokes bitchery in the first place. Hannah, who is fifteen, says that sometimes she just longs for others to be honest. 'There's this girl with monkey ears and I know she had them pinned back surgically so I used to play around with her hair and pull it back and look at her ears. It was really mean of me and I really regret it now but I just wanted her to admit that she had had it done.'

Once we can acknowledge that women are human and allowed to get angry, we are less hard on ourselves, and more honest. We don't have to be selfless and kind, we should get cross when people offend us. If someone says or does something to upset or undermine you, summon up the strength to say so to their face at the time, without judgement. It will clear the air, allow them the space to apologise and you will both be able to move on. It isn't easy I know, the tendency is always to avoid rather than confront. But avoidance leads to resentment and with resentment comes bitchery. It takes confidence and a quickness of mind to recognise when something has made you angry, but when you manage it once, you will recognise how refreshing that is and find the confidence to do it again.

Why It's Important to be Loud

When we conform to age-old stereotypes of what a woman should be – the kind and compassionate carer and mother; the attractive, slim, sexually hot soulmate who always understands what a man needs; the adept multi-tasker; the placid, selfless, brain-dead appeaser; the 'Good Girl'; the 'Wronged Woman'; the 'Bitch' – we are not being true to ourselves. Women are a glorious powerhouse of originality, strengths and talents that are largely untapped because we are often so consumed by trying to be what we think we should be rather than true to ourselves.

These stereotypes belittle and disempower us. 'Good', self-less girls don't speak out, they take everything on the chin and expect other women to be continuously kind, never cruel. What a recipe for disappointment. 'Good' girls don't get the jobs they want because they expect to be offered them rather than fighting for them and they never get that pay rise because they're too scared to ask. 'Good' girls do the bulk of the housework and the childcare because they feel that's what 'good' mothers do. And then when other men or women are horrid to them, because human beings of both sexes can be deeply cruel, the 'good' girl risks becoming the victim. She absorbs the abuse that comes from being bitched about by other girls at school, assumes it must be her fault or something she's done and the ability to identify an abusive relationship is lost. She enters the danger zone, liable to grow into a woman who becomes the punchbag for men's fists, unable to leave. It's OK to be the 'Bad' girl sometimes. The danger of the 'Good Girl' paradigm is that there is nothing in between the 'nice' where anything considered negative or angry is suppressed and 'bitch', where it all comes out, and how.

'Good' girls depend upon the approval and praise of others, always the child looking for love. It is only with a sense of autonomy and self-respect that we can command that respect from others. That means having the confidence to be yourself. So make a stand. Nobody is going to just give you what you want in life unless you go out and ask for it, unless you speak your mind honestly and forcefully. It's only by speaking out and having the confidence to express your opinions honestly that others will see you for who you are rather than what you wear or who you hang out with. Say it loud. Say it often. Expect to be heard. You're allowed to get angry, daily. There's a lot to be angry about. Engage with and rage at the injustices in the world rather than at the minor irritations of individual women. And if others disagree with you, so be it. Perhaps they have a point. Through discourse there is dialogue and the potential for greater knowledge and change.

If we resist the pressure to be the 'good' girl there is greater room in our lives for our own needs. We don't have to be more *selfish* in the sense of riding roughshod over other people, but less *selfless* in that what you want and think matters most. You do not have to always put others first – as the actress Katharine Hepburn once said, 'If you always do what interests you, at least one person will be pleased.' You only have one life and a key aspect to success in anything is not trying to please everybody else all of the time. The 'good' girl wants to be liked more than she wants to be heard. But isn't it better to be admired and respected as a powerful woman by those whom you yourself respect than considered that vapid, insipid girl who allows others to make the decisions and apologises regularly for her existence?

When we lack the confidence to live the lives we want, we envy what others have. Jealousy is at the core of most women's bitching. Instead of using our envy to identify what we want and then going for it, we bitch about others who have succeeded and try and trip them up. Author Rachel Oakes-Ash calls this the Skipping Theory. 'The girls on either end are completely passive, and the girl in the middle is jumping over the rope. If she's good she can skip for ages while the girls holding the rope are waiting for her to make a mistake so that they can have a turn. In order to do that they might make the rope swing faster to trip her up. I think this is what we carry with us as women for the rest of our lives. Most of us believe there is only one slice of the pie and only one spotlight and only one woman can have that at a time. And if *you* have it, I'm standing passively by trying to trip you up. Whereas with boys the guy that passes the ball to get the goal is applauded just as much as the person who scored it.'

We compete now with men as well as with other women

so the sooner we learn how to do it well, the higher our chances of achieving our ambitions. It's OK to want to do well. You only have one life and no one is going to hand you everything you desire on a platter. You have to identify what it is you want from life and go out and get it. If you put the destructive female tendency of needing to please others above the need to look after yourself, you will always feel small and inadequate. You do not hurt others by striving for what you want; you only hurt yourself if you allow your feelings for others to stop you from identifying how to fulfil your own desires. When you feel envy or jealousy towards someone use those emotions positively to focus on what you really want from life. When other people succeed at something it means you can too. Stop comparing yourself to other people, it's not like being in a race where only one person can win – you have a unique life path and can use your inherent competitive drive to push you on.

You can change the way you view competition by seeing it as setting yourself challenges rather than defeating others. To compete effectively you have to improve your skills and turn your weaknesses into strengths and as that happens confidence builds, genuine confidence in what you can do rather than how you look. Play family games at home with family and friends who won't mind if you win. Get involved in team games where you can be allowed to feel the urge to win and stop talking about your failures. Try saying 'I'm good at . . .' for a change.

There will always be someone more successful, beautiful, richer than you are to envy and there will be things that others envy in you. When you feel envious of something that someone has, think of all the assets and advantages you have that others don't. If you feel a deep and prolonged jealousy of a close friend be open and honest about it with her, talk about why you feel this way, because the chances are she envies something you have or feels deeply insecure or unhappy about something else that you've never even considered. Try saying how pleased you are for her when something nice happens, 'You really deserve it,' is the nicest thing a friend can say because you are sharing in the joy of her triumph, rather than making her feel guilty about expressing her pleasure at success. If you talk openly about jealousy with friends, and go into the areas of greatest conflict between you, you make your friendship stronger in those places and there is less of a need to bitch about them behind their backs.

When we are criticised for something and feel vulnerable as a result, it is hard not to feel as if one's whole being is under attack. But it isn't. When someone disagrees with you, or a teacher criticises an essay, it's the essay under discussion not everything else about you. If we disentangle our lives into millions of tiny separate threads, it is easier to see criticism for what it is – another perspective provoking thought and discussion which ultimately leads to improvement. If you want to succeed at anything, you have to develop a firm enough sense of self to withstand criticism in order to be able to improve your performance and progress.

Good relationships are not threatened by disagreements. We need to learn how to agree to disagree, for it is difference and debate that teaches us how to stick up for what we value and believe in and affirm our sense of self. And with a firmer sense of ourselves as individuals we feel more secure with our advantages and feel less jealous. We feel more able to compete out there in what can seem like an overwhelmingly competitive world and we bitch about each other less.